Inside the
Large Congregation

Inside the
Large Congregation

SUSAN BEAUMONT

The Alban Institute
Herndon, Virginia

The Alban Institute
2121 Cooperative Way, Suite 100
Herndon, VA 20171

Cover design by Tobias Becker, Bird Box Design

Cover image from Plymouth United Church of Christ in Des Moines, Iowa, taken by John Schultz.

Library of Congress Cataloging-in-Publication Data

Beaumont, Susan.
  Inside the large congregation / Susan Beaumont.
      p. cm.
  Includes bibliographical references and index.
  ISBN 978-1-56699-419-4 (alk. paper)
  1. Big churches. I. Title.
  BV637.9.B43 2011
  250--dc23
                        2011034125

11   12   13   14   15   VG   5   4   3   2   1

Contents

Foreword by Lewis Galloway   vii
Preface   xi
Acknowledgements   xix

Part 1: Size Does Matter

1. Why Size Matters: The Large Church in Context   3
2. How Size Changes Things   23
3. Living Large: Exploring Large Church Size Categories   43

Part 2: Leadership Systems in Motion

4. Clergy Leadership Roles   73
5. Staff Team Design and Function   111
6. Governance and Board Function   139
7. Acculturation and Engagement of the Laity   171
8. Forming and Executing Strategy   193

Epilogue   235
Notes   239

124157

Foreword

WHEN I WAS A COLLEGE STUDENT, I PARTICIPATED IN A PROGRAM WHERE I spent my junior year abroad in Europe. I remember the experience of exploring for the first time the city where I would spend a year. At first, everything appeared to be different: the voices on the street, the food in the markets and restaurants, the classes at the university, the transportation system, and even the interactions among the people. I felt as if I had entered a strange new world. Gradually the strange became familiar, and I began to understand, appreciate, and delight in the differences.

Coming to a large church as a new pastor or lay leader can be like entering a strange new world. Even if we have been in a congregation for some years, we may suddenly realize that the congregation is not same as it once was. Something has changed, and we can't quite put our finger on the differences. The congregation may be larger or smaller, more tired or more energetic, and facing new controversies or new leadership challenges. We suddenly realize that things don't work like they used to work. It is hard to get things done, to communicate, to define staff roles, to secure volunteers, to make new plans, and to acculturate new members. *Inside the Large Congregation* names the differences.

Inside the Large Congregation is a carefully researched and thoughtful guide to understanding and addressing the particular dynamics of various sized large churches. Susan Beaumont brings to the task her personal experiences in large congregations, her training and background in business and theology, and her outstanding work as a consultant with large congregations.

Congregational size matters not only in how small, medium, large, and mega churches operate, but also within the category of the large church. This work addresses congregations that have between 400 and 2000 in attendance on Sunday mornings. She gives us the language to talk about the nuanced differences that churches face as they reach the threshold of becoming large churches and as they move within the various types of large churches. Describing the characteristics of the multi-cell congregation on the verge of becoming a large church, the professional church, the strategic church, and the matrix church enables congregational leaders not only to analyze their own situations but also to engage in helpful conversations about their congregations. She ends each chapter with probing questions for analysis and discussion. Beaumont succeeds admirably in her goal of assisting pastors and lay leaders in the task of tending to the various dynamic systems within the church to foster healthy congregational life and mission.

Through her work as a consultant, Susan Beaumont has identified what she names as five basic leadership systems that can be found in every large church: the leadership role of the clergy, the design and function of the staff team, the governing function of the board, the role and acculturation of the laity, and the development and execution of long range strategy. The second part of the book is a careful analysis of how each of these five systems should function in each type of large congregations. These systems function differently according to the size of the congregation. As congregations grow, develop new ministries, face new challenges, or even shrink, these leadership systems must also change in order to continue to function effectively in the life of the church. Beaumont gives useful concrete examples of the dynamic interplay of how changing congregational size and changing leadership systems can impact each other in helpful and unhelpful ways. The key to healthy, vibrant congregational life is to have these five leadership systems functioning in ways that are appropriate to the needs of that particular size congregation. The five leadership systems need to be in alignment with the size of the large congregation.

The second part of the book examines these leadership systems in motion and will be of interest to both clergy and laity. Lay leaders may find the chapters on effective board form and governance, assimilating and engaging members in ministry, and strategic planning to be of particular interest. In reflecting on board governance, some familiarity with the Alban book, *Governance and Ministry: Rethinking Board Leadership* by Dan Hotchkiss, is helpful as background for Beaumont's discussion on board form and function. Even if the polity or theology of a particular ecclesiastical tradition is not particularly compatible with her suggestions for effective board governance, her concepts can be an effective tool for analyzing the governance of any congregation. In welcoming new members into the large congregation, she makes a helpful distinction between assimilation and the more appropriate concept of acculturation. I appreciate the emphasis that Beaumont places on the importance of the governing boards of large congregations giving sufficient time, attention, and energy to strategic planning.

In addition to the leadership systems mentioned above, clergy and staff professionals will also find the chapters on the role of clergy and the design and function of staff teams to be very valuable. Beaumont provides a realistic and sensitive discussion of how the role of clergy in large churches changes depending upon the position (pastor, executive pastor, associate pastor, specialized ministry) and the size of the congregation. She gives a thoughtful summary of the essential skills and functions of the various clergy roles and ministry contexts. She highlights how the interaction and responsibilities of the staff and members shift as large churches grow and change.

Large churches are not better than small churches. They are just different. No matter what size the particular congregation may be, all churches have gifts and challenges. *Inside the Large Congregation* gives the pastors, staff, and lay leaders of large churches the opportunity and tools to reflect upon the practice of ministry in order to become healthier, more effective, and more faithful congregations. It is Susan Beaumont's desire to help the leaders of large churches find "grace in the journey."

Lewis F. Galloway
Second Presbyterian Church
Indianapolis, Indiana

Preface

I BEGAN MY WORK AS A SENIOR CONSULTANT WITH THE ALBAN INSTITUTE in 2005, with the understanding that I would develop my practice to address the unique needs of the large congregation. At that time *large* was still fairly undefined in the minds of those who hired me. Alban selected me for this work because I had some life experience in large congregations and because I had a rather unusual blend of backgrounds in corporate America and in congregational systems, a background that Alban thought would lend itself well to working with the complexity of large congregations. I was to use my dual business school and divinity degrees to evaluate the best of business practices, filtered through a theological lens, to determine what might fit and what wouldn't fit in the world of congregations. To that end, my work over the past five years has been about trying to give voice to the organizational and leadership demands of large congregations.

As I began my work with Alban, I was struck by the number of requests from large congregations asking, "How is _____ (staffing, governance, planning, pastoral transition) supposed to work for a church our size?" Some variation on this theme seemed to drive every request for help that Alban received from large congregations. Initially I assumed that someone somewhere had researched and answered questions about large church organizational effectiveness. My job, I thought, was to figure out where that information resided, so that I could apply that knowledge to my practice. And so, I began to read and to research.

OTHER VOICES

Early thinking about congregational size and its impact on organization was shaped by Arlin Rothauge's "Sizing Up a Congregation for New Member Ministry," published in 1983. The primary focus of the publication was to help church leaders target their evangelism efforts appropriately, based upon the size of the congregation they were serving. Interestingly, the evangelical component of that publication has dropped from view while the piece of the work that dealt with the unique cultural and leadership dimensions of different sized congregations has remained with us. Rothauge defined four types of congregations that he labeled the family church (fewer than 50 people in average worship attendance), the pastoral church (50-150 in average worship attendance), the program church (150-350 in average worship attendance), and the corporation church (more than 350 in average worship attendance). His work rested on the premise that there are different leadership and relational patterns, and consequently different cultures that operate in different sized congregations.

Rothauge's seminal piece has produced an overall understanding that congregational size (in addition to life cycle and context) is a key determinant in how a church needs to be organized and led. The three smallest size designations he coined have remained the definitive labels for small and medium sized congregations. However, over time the *corporation* label has been challenged. Congregations, no matter how large, never really function like corporations due to the covenantal nature of the relationships that stand at the center of congregational life. The term *resource congregations* has been bantered about as a replacement for the corporate label first assigned by Rothauge. Many prefer this label because it captures the capacity for excellence and the "resource rich" image of the large congregation. While the resource label may make some more comfortable, it doesn't bring us to any better understanding of the size category. Some have argued that the threshold for large church size begins around 400 (not the 350 barrier that Rothauge identified). Many have wondered about the upper limit of the *corporation* size label. Can a church that is 800, 1000 or 1,200 be captured adequately by the characterization of a single label?

In 1999 Gary McIntosh published *One Size Doesn't Fit All,* in which he coined new language that gave voice to the challenge of becoming large. McIntosh referred to the Small church (15–200 worshipers) as a relational single cell, the Medium church (201–400 worshipers) as the programmatic stretched cell, and the Large Church (more than 400 worshipers) as the organizational multiple cell. The stretched cell that eventually gives way to a multi-celled structure provides rich imagery for congregations as they do the difficult work of making the medium- to large-church size transition. McIntosh was able to articulate specific factors that a congregation needs to adapt when making the size transition from medium to large: where the center of authority resides, pastoral decision-making style, staff size, who manages the change process, growth patterns, growth obstacles, and growth strategies. However, McIntosh's work (at that time) stopped at churches with 400 in average worship attendance.

In 2000 Lyle Schaller wrote *The Very Large Church*, in which he explored the cultural implications and organizational challenges of congregations with worshipping communities between 750 and 1,800. Schaller highlighted the presence of key size transition points around 800 and again around 1,800 in worship and some of the unique leadership dynamics that existed in leading a congregation between these transition zones. He did not seek to name or codify the transition points nor explain how to manage them, beyond drawing our attention to their existence and significance.

In 2007 Scott Thumma and Dave Travis of the Leadership Network undertook a significant research project to explore the cultural boom in the emergence of megachurches (more than 2,000 in weekly worship attendance). In *Beyond Megachurch Myths,* the authors explored the cultural landscape that gave birth to the megachurch, and they addressed some of the organizational dimensions of these largest institutions.

Throughout this period of time (1983-2007), the notion that size matters in understanding the organizational complexity and leadership of a congregation remained firmly entrenched. People widely understand that the organizational dynamics of the large church are significantly different from the dynamics of smaller congregations and that large church leaders must master different skill sets. However, specific structures and processes for leading congregations that are large, but not mega, still remain largely unexplored. In the end, none of the existing literature provided clarity on how I might lead my client base toward better organizational health.

RECOGNIZING THE PATTERNS

In my first several years with Alban, I stumbled around with gracious congregations that hired me as we tried together to articulate the organizational challenges of the large church, and as I attempted to begin speaking authoritatively about how to address those challenges. My corporate consulting background, in some ways, suited me to tackle their challenges, once we could articulate what the real issues were. Articulating the real issues was the difficult part.

After several years of mucking around in the problems of large churches, I began to identify an organizing framework for making sense out of the problems that large congregations were facing. In most instances some part of the leadership system within each client congregation was out of sync with other parts of the system. Perhaps the governing board was doing well in its task of governance, but there was frustration with how the staff team was organized. In other situations the staff team felt high functioning, but they were being micromanaged by a well-intentioned board that couldn't seem to find its core purpose. In still others the senior pastor was on the brink of collapse after years of moving the organization through sheer force of will and personality, working with an organizational infrastructure that was sorely underdeveloped. Many times a request for help with planning actually masked another systemic problem that needed to be addressed.

Initially, all of these challenges seemed related, but not directly connected. I was organizing my consulting practice around independent consulting interventions that addressed specific presenting issues: staffing, governance, planning, and pastoral transition. Then I began to ponder the relationship between the different kinds of interventions I was frequently called to engage. I began to view the variety of leadership challenges I saw in large congregations as part of a singular whole. Clients invited me to enter their systems from different vantage points, depending upon the most pressing presenting symptom or problem, but almost all of the consultations dealt with some aspect of getting organizationally aligned.

In a moment of clarity (in an airplane, poised somewhere over the Midwest, where most of my moments of great clarity seem to take place), I realized that everything I was working on with congregations came down to five basic leadership systems that needed to stay in alignment for the large church to function well for its size:

1. Clergy leadership roles
2. Staff team design and function
3. Governance and board function
4. Acculturation and the role of laity
5. Forming and executing strategy

Furthermore, I noticed that these five systems operated with some important but subtle distinctions in the emerging large church (400–800 in worship attendance), the established large church (800–1,200), and the very large church (1,200–2,000). It was becoming clear to me that many of my clients' problems were related to the fact that one or more of the five systems were inappropriately structured for the size of their congregation. In other words, the church wasn't acting its size. The presenting problems in most of my consultations had something to do with leaders functioning in a system that was better suited for a different sized congregation. And so, I began trying to articulate how the five systems worked in tandem in different sized large congregations. And I began paying attention to what triggered the need to transition from one organizational framework of these five systems into the next.

In 2008 I wrote an article that was published in *Congregations* magazine entitled "Beyond Corporate: New Insights on Larger Churches." In that article I articulated a new typology for thinking about size in the large congregation. I labeled the three categories mentioned earlier and characterized how the five systems worked distinctively in each of those three categories. After the article was published, pastors and board leaders began calling for help because the model that I had presented in the article made intuitive sense to them. Since that publication I have made a variety of changes to the typology, and I have added an additional size category.

In 2009 Gary McIntosh published *Taking Your Church to the Next Level,* in which he coined some of his own names for the larger end of the size range in congregations. McIntosh's work is largely about the intersection of congregational life cycle and size theory. His book is unapologetically a church growth book that focuses on tending to cycles of fruitfulness and decline across all sizes of congregations. Although his focus is not exclusively on the large congregation, it is encouraging to me that his work has led him to name size transition zones that are remarkably in sync with the categories I've been using in my work.

WHAT THIS BOOK SEEKS TO ACCOMPLISH

This book is about the church that is more than mid-sized and not quite mega, the congregation with an average weekend worshiping community between 400 and 2,000. This is not a church growth book. It explores organizational and leadership dynamics that may prevent health and growth from happening, but it does not advocate for numerical growth or predict when growth will happen. This book does not assume that large is better than mid-sized or small; it does assume that the large church functions dramatically differently from the megachurch, mid-sized, or small congregation.

This book seeks to articulate why size matters and how it matters in the world of large congregations. Historically all churches larger than mid-size and not quite mega have been viewed through the same organizational and leadership lens. This book seeks to flesh out the nuances of moving across the 400 to 2,000 average attendance range.

I am invested in helping large congregations "rightsize" their leadership systems to better serve their ministry contexts. For some congregations this simply means getting all of their leadership systems to work in support of the size category that they have been living in for a number of years. For other congregations this means downsizing systems that were designed for an earlier era when the congregation was much larger than it is today. And for still others it is about preparing to enter a larger size category.

This is meant to be a practical text, to help congregational leaders identify what needs to happen today and tomorrow to more effectively lead their congregations. It can be used diagnostically to help leaders more clearly identify the challenges they are facing. It can be used as a dialogue tool, providing labels and common language to help leadership groups come to a joint understanding about their own landscape. In that sense it is meant to provide a model for large church leadership that is both descriptive (where are we now?) and prescriptive (what do we do next?)

The first part of this book, "Size Does Matter," will explore the various ways in which size impacts leadership dynamics. Chapter 1 is an exploration of the large church in context, our ambivalence about large congregations, and their strengths and challenges. Chapter 2 examines how size changes things, the basic building blocks of congregations, and the five leadership systems that hold those building blocks together. Chapter 3 lays out a size typology and explores three size categories within the spectrum of "large," defining the transition zones when a congregation moves from one organizational orientation to another.

Part Two of the book is "Leadership Systems in Motion." A separate chapter is devoted to each of the five major leadership systems in large congregations that shift during predictable transition zones. Chapter 4 will explore clergy leadership roles. Chapter 5 will focus on staff team design and function. Chapter 6 is about board design and governance. Chapter 7 addresses acculturation and the role of laity. And chapter 8 is about forming and executing strategy. Various group diagnostic tools and discussion guidelines will be provided to help congregations explore how their size and their structure influence leadership effectiveness.

This book is written for anyone who wants to better understand the leadership and organizational dynamics of the large church. It is appropriate for heads of staff, pastoral leaders, program leaders, administrative leaders, lay leaders, seminarians, and denominational executives—anyone seeking to understand the challenges of leading from *Inside the Large Congregation.*

Acknowledgements

This book contains many stories of congregations and their leaders. All of the stories represent real life struggles and events of congregations that have invited me into their lives over the past six years. Names, locations, and key identifying factors have been changed to provide anonymity. In some instances stories were merged or simplified to more effectively illustrate a concept.

I am forever grateful to the many congregations and leaders who have allowed me to walk with them as consultant or coach. Every one of you (and you know who you are) has in some way informed this text. A handful of congregations, listed below, have been particularly instrumental in shaping my understanding of large church dynamics. These congregations have graciously invited me to walk with them over a period of months (and even years in some instances). In-depth interaction with the leaders of these congregations has allowed me to formulate and test my theories about large church leadership. I have been sharpened by the honesty of your questions, the power of your insights, the transparency of your struggles, and your passion for ministry. Thank you!

All Souls Unitarian Universalist, New York NY
Bryn Mawr Presbyterian, Bryn Mawr PA
Canterbury United Methodist Church, Birmingham AL
First Community Church, Columbus OH
Foundry United Methodist, Washington DC
Geist Christian, Indianapolis IN
Independent Presbyterian Church, Birmingham AL

Johns Creek Baptist Church, Alpharetta GA
Los Altos United Methodist Church, Los Altos CA
Myers Park Baptist Church, Charlotte NC
Plymouth Congregational Church (UCC), Des Moines IA
Preston Hollow Presbyterian Church, Dallas TX

I owe a debt of gratitude to my colleagues around the Alban table who have been instrumental in sharpening this material. Alice Mann, and her incredible work on the pastoral to program size transition, laid important groundwork out of which this book grows. Dan Hotchkiss, and his writings on governance and ministry, coined important language that weaves its way through the last three chapters of this text. Richard Bass helped to shape early book outlines. The manuscript was pruned and made immeasurably better by the inspired editing work of Beth Gaede and the careful copyediting of Lauren Belen. Twila Glenn, Susan Nienaber, Larry Peers, and Bob Leventhal provided encouragement, support and feedback across a two year span of writing and editing.

Finally, I thank the friends and loved ones who sustain me and fuel my passion for the work; especially my four favorite men: my husband Bruce and my sons Chris, Matt, and Jon.

PART 1

Size Does Matter

CHAPTER 1

Why Size Matters
The Large Church in Context

WHAT ARE THE CENTRAL ESSENTIAL CHARACTERISTICS THAT MAKE THIS congregation unique? This is a question that I frequently pose to congregations who engage me as their consultant. Healthy congregations know who they are and how they are different from other congregations. A healthy congregation might respond with something like this: "We are a congregation that values excellence in worship and the arts. We have a progressive theology and are known for our commitment to the pursuit of social justice." Or, "We are proud of our intergenerational approach to faith formation and development. We excel in offering a strong Sunday school program and a vibrant small group ministry that thrive side by side."

Recently, leaders of a congregation that I worked with posed this question to their members as part of a series of listening circles. A disturbing phenomenon surfaced as we began reviewing the collected data. A significant number of people responded to the question about central essential characteristics by replying with some version of, "Well, I guess what makes us unique is that we are big." These statements about the size of the congregation were often made without any qualifiers about why big was important or what it helped the congregation to accomplish. People simply thought that what made them unique was their size. Size was an end unto itself.

As we probed the responses a little further, we discovered that people meant many different things when they named size as an essential characteristic of the congregation. Some talked about the fact that the size of the congregation generated enough resources to ensure that the congregation could make an impact in its community. For others, size produced a capacity for excellence in worship and education that they valued. For still others, the size of the congregation was a measure of prestige. They valued being part of the "biggest and richest" congregation around. (Leaders expressed a collective "ouch" in response to that last interpretation.)

As you can imagine, this data produced some interesting dialogue among leaders. Is size an end unto itself—or a means to accomplish something else? If we cease to be a large and resource rich congregation, will we have failed in our mission? Should our size be one of the core values expressed by our congregation? What difference does it really make that we are considered "big" in the world of congregations? What does our size allow us to accomplish?

AMBIVALENCE ABOUT LARGE

Does God care about the size of our faith communities? Our scriptural heritage is full of stories about how size doesn't matter. Joseph, the youngest of Jacob's sons, saved his family and a future nation from a great famine. David, the smallest of eight brothers, killed Goliath. A remnant few reestablished the nation of Israel after the exile. A small band of 12 committed disciples infected the world with the Gospel of Jesus Christ. You might say that our Judeo-Christian heritage has a bias towards the small, the marginalized, and the insignificant. One biblical story after another reinforces the notion that size and significance have nothing to do with impact and redemption. God chooses those who are small and underprivileged, by the world's standards, to accomplish great things.

Given our scriptural heritage, it is no wonder that many Christians are skeptical about large institutions and structures. People love stories about small, struggling, undercapitalized groups that rise up to accomplish great things. Justice is served when the glory of God shines through the ministry of a scrappy group of people who refuse to believe that they are insignificant, people who know, at the center of their being, that with God on their side anything is possible.

During our most recent economic recession, politicians and theologians alike delighted in pitting Wall Street against Main Street, a powerful metaphor meant to expose the insatiable, self-serving appetites of large institutions. Similarly, endless debates have ensued about the growing size of our national, state, and local governments, warning that the larger an institutional body becomes, the less likely it is to effectively serve the genuine needs of the people.

Paradoxically, even as we criticize our largest institutions, we continue to shift attention and buying dollars towards larger shopping venues, larger entertainment venues, and larger vehicles. Hospitals, schools, stores, factories, and entertainment centers have all grown to mega-proportions. As we lambaste large institutions, we continue to behave in ways that support larger institutional life. Let's face it. Culturally we are ambivalent about institutional size. We appreciate the resources and market efficiencies that large institutions produce for us, but we are skeptical about their moral value and their importance in our lives.

It's safe to say that ambivalence about institutional size extends itself to the life of the church. Megachurches and large multi-site churches are changing the landscape of North American religion. Pastoral leaders, denominational leaders, church consultants, and seminaries are increasingly focusing their attention on the phenomenon of the megachurch and trying to figure out what the long-term viability of the movement amounts to, how megachurches are changing the practice of American religion, and whether they represent a threat or boon to the institutional church.

Whatever ambivalence people feel toward the large church, the large church is a growing phenomenon. America has seen an explosion in the number of megachurches over the past three decades. An examination of population and megachurch growth reveals that the number of megachurches is increasing exponentially per capita. From 1980 to 2010, the number of megachurches per million of population doubled every ten years.[1] With few exceptions, it is estimated that there is a megachurch within a ninety-minute drive of 80 percent of the US population.[2] Whatever suspicions our culture bears about the authenticity of the megachurch, it is speaking to, and serving, a growing segment of our population.

While we watch the continued proliferation of very large churches, many people challenge the nature of the gospel they proclaim and the nature of the community they promote. Do they compromise and dumb down the gospel to appeal to wider audiences, offering easy-to-believe prosperity messages that are designed to offend no one? Do people experience authentic discipleship, and is the flock adequately shepherded? Do they confuse entertainment and worship? Are mega-congregations built around the charisma of a pastoral leader instead of a firm biblical foundation? People are skeptical about the growing presence of the megachurch within the world of congregations.

In response to the phenomenon of the very large church, critics draw attention back to the sustaining presence of the small church on the American landscape. We are reminded that most congregations are small. The median congregation has only 75 regularly participating people and an annual budget of approximately $90,000. Ninety percent of all congregations have on average 350 or fewer attendees. Despite the proliferation of the megachurch, the size of the average congregation has not changed since 1998.[3] The small church continues to represent a tenacious presence on the religious landscape, and some would argue it is a purer expression of the gospel.

The 2006-2007 National Congregations Study draws attention to this important fact: Even though most congregations in the United States are small, most people are in large congregations. The average person is in a congregation with 400 people and a budget of $280,000.[4] Consider this illustration from the study:

> To get a feel for just how concentrated people are in the largest congregations, imagine that we have lined up all congregations in the United States, from the smallest to the largest. Imagine that you are walking up this line, starting with the smallest. When you get to a congregation with 400 people, you would

have walked past about half of all churchgoers, but more than 90 percent of all congregations! Or imagine walking down this line of congregations from the other direction, starting with the very largest. When you get to that same 400-person congregation, you would have walked past only 10 percent of all congregations but half of all churchgoers.[5]

The movement of people from smaller to larger churches is not merely a megachurch phenomenon. Large mainline congregations (between 350 and 2,000 in worship attendance) are growing in size and importance along with the megachurch. The Faith Communities Today Survey, conducted by the Hartford Institute of Religion Research in 2000, revealed that congregations with more than 350 members have been growing at a significantly faster rate than smaller congregations.[6]

Table 1.1   Congregational Growth, 1995–2000

OLDLINE PROTESTANT*

Number of regularly participating adults	Percent of congregations growing by 5% or more
1 thru 49	30%
50 thru 99	41%
100 thru 149	52%
150 thru 349	50%
350 thru 999	70%
1000 or More	66%

EVANGELICAL PROTESTANT*

Number of regularly participating adults	Percent of congregations growing by 5% or more
1 thru 49	37%
50 thru 99	50%
100 thru 149	60%
150 thru 349	66%
350 thru 999	74%
1000 or More	83%

* Does not include historic black denominations

Although the large (between mid-size and mega) Protestant church does not suffer quite the same stigma as the evangelical megachurch, it elicits its fair share of ambivalent reaction. Consider:

- In most denominational systems pastoral leadership in the large church is more highly compensated than pastoral leadership in small to mid-sized congregations. The operating budget of the large church can sustain higher salary levels. By default, large congregations are viewed as peak vocational assignments. Most pastors strive to move into progressively larger congregations with each vocational move, however, they are often ambivalent about the shift in pastoral focus that goes along with leadership in the larger church. (More will be said about this focus in chapter 4 on clergy leadership roles). Outstanding pastoral leadership in small church environments is never recognized as being on par with outstanding pastoral leadership in the large church, and this is problematic.
- Large church pastors often project significant charisma and leadership presence. Often, though, the persona and ego strength of the large church pastor are viewed with suspicion. Does the charisma and ego strength serve the church well?
- Denominational systems have a love-hate relationship with their largest congregations. The large congregation is often the most significant funder of regional denominational work, which means that it typically wields larger say than the average sized congregation in denominational decision making. This is offensive to the leaders of many smaller congregations.
- Denominational leaders can serve the most people by concentrating their attention on just the largest churches, but that strategy would leave the majority of congregations out of the picture. Consequently, most denominational programs and systems are set up to serve the average church and do not meet the needs of the largest congregations.

This results in larger congregations going their own way on polity and practice issues, which can be offensive to other congregations, and other pastoral and denominational leaders.

My Own Ambivalence

Before I can expect you to buy into my perspectives on the strengths and weaknesses of large congregations, I think it only fair that I share my own personal history with the large church and to claim my own sense of ambivalence. I often invite clients that I work with to reflect upon the size congregation that they belonged to when they first seriously engaged their own faith. This is not necessarily the church that they grew up in; it is the church they were in when they first became spiritually alive or actively engaged with God. I ask this question because I often find that the church that people come of age in becomes their benchmark for how church "ought to function." The way that the pastor of that congregation led becomes a standard against which all subsequent pastors are evaluated. The function of the staff team in that church becomes the right way to organize a staff team in their mind. Helping leaders to rightsize their congregational structures often requires getting leaders to examine unstated assumptions that they carry around in their heads about how the church ought to function and what size it ought to be. These unstated assumptions are often associated with the congregation in which they had their foundational faith awakening experience.

I came of age spiritually in a large Roman Catholic church. The congregation that my family and I belonged to boasted a membership base of 3,000 families. My brothers and I attended a parochial school attached to the church, and I was one of one hundred fifty kids in my grade level in that school. The church was big by any measure.

With this experience as my foundational faith experience, I find that I move easily in and among large congregations. I feel naturally at home there. I love the organizational complexity of large congregations. I love their capacity for excellence in worship, music, and programming. I am drawn to the diversity they attract and the depth of programming they can offer. I intuitively resonate with the structures and leadership systems of the large congregation.

I have journeyed far afield since those early days. I am no longer Roman Catholic but call the American Baptist denomination my home. I have served on the staff team of a nondenominational megachurch, and I have served as the interim pastor of a pastoral sized Baptist congregation. I have been employed on a regional denominational staff where I moved in and among congregations of all sizes. Today, as a consultant to congregations, I find myself inextricably drawn back to life and ministry in large congregations.

At the same time, I often find the large congregation off-putting. The anonymity that large congregations offer sometimes attracts a membership base that is minimally engaged in their faith and community. Many of the client systems I work with are both large and affluent. Something is fundamentally distasteful to me about people who join a faith community because it is resource rich; because it offers the best in programming entertainment, music, and worship; because it is the place where "everyone who is anyone attends;" or because they themselves can support mission and ministry without getting their own hands dirty.

The large church has the capacity to make an impact, and to be bold, excellent, cutting edge, missional, shallow, sterile, obsessed with size for size's sake, prestigious, and arrogant . . . all at the same time. For better or worse I am drawn to the dynamics of the large congregation, and I have staked my professional ministry life in this arena.

It is not my intent in this book to advocate on behalf of the large congregation or to argue against it. I do not seek to provide a biblical, theological, or ecclesiastical argument for or against the large church. The large church is. It represents a phenomenon that seems to be growing in importance. We need to better understand it—what it offers, how it functions, and how to create organizational and leadership systems that serve it well. Readers will have to come to terms with their own ambivalence about large congregational systems. This book will not help you in that regard. It will help you understand what "leading large" requires.

In the remainder of this chapter we will explore our collective attraction to the large congregation and the inherent limitations that sometimes prevent it from effectively serving the very culture that finds it so attractive.

OUR ATTRACTION TO LARGE

Exactly what is it that makes the large church particularly attractive in this cultural era? In the paragraphs that follow we will explore five major themes that create a sense of appeal for the large church in this day and age. The reader will see that it is not only what the large church has to offer that makes it so attractive, but also how it offers itself.

Capacity for Excellence

Why is the large church growing in numbers and importance? Lyle Schaller offers this explanation. We live in a high expectation culture. Increasingly, people are looking for congregations with a threefold emphasis on relevance, quality, and choices. Increasingly people are seeking congregations that:

- Excel in presenting the gospel in what is perceived as relevant terms (bridging the experience of faith and life). Increasingly this requires the use of technology (see below) and greater diversity in expressions of worship and programming.
- Carry a reputation for high quality in worship, teaching, training, and other aspects of congregational life.
- Provide people with a broad range of attractive choices in worship, learning, involvement in ministry, facilitating the individual personal spiritual pilgrimage, helping rear their children, and finding a sense of community.

A generous estimate is that only one-fifth of today's Protestant congregations can mobilize the resources required to meet all three of these expectations.[7] This is fragile ground on which to stand. It is not meant to suggest that small congregations can't be relevant and offer quality preaching and teaching and diverse choices. However, if the benchmark for excellence is the presence of all three features simultaneously, the resource-richer large congregation is at a decided advantage.

Effective Use of Technology

The 1990s brought about a technological revolution equivalent in significance to the invention of movable-type printing press in the fifteenth century. Culturally we have shifted from communication that is printed and spoken to communication that is visually supported with imagery, motion, humor, drama, and music. This shift is transforming the worship service from what has traditionally been a low-energy, verbal presentation style to higher energy, multi-media, and entertaining worship experiences.[8] The use of visual projection in worship has more than doubled in the past decade. Additionally, website development in congregations has also more than doubled in the past decade, and the use of e-mail has almost tripled.[9] Technology is clearly influencing the way we do church.

Overall, large congregations have greater resource capacity to purchase and use technology effectively, which contributes to their sense of cultural relevance. One need only look at the staffing structure of a typical large congregation to see the capacity for using technology. A typical large church staff team includes a director of communications (code for person in charge of website management and electronic communication) and an information technology professional (one who maintains computers, databases, and so forth). In the more contemporary large church, the director of visual arts and technology has replaced the work that used to be done by the minister of music.

In the large church the people who operate technology during worship services are often paid staff with developed expertise, to ensure that technology usage is seamless. When professionalism in technology is absent, the worship service can be painfully held hostage while some well-intentioned but poorly equipped volunteer tries to get the slides to advance along with the music or preaching.

Finally, the presence of technology is giving way to a new organizational expression of church referred to as the multi-site church. The multi-site church frequently makes use of video technology to create linkages between worship and ministry sites. This emergent form of church is allowing growing congregations to continue expanding in ways that are not limited by building and parking capacity. The large church, with its ability to manage complexity, is better equipped to manage multi-site ministry. The decentralized and matrix organizational structures needed to support multi-site ministry are more natural to the culture of the large congregation.

Space for Anonymity and Intimacy

In his groundbreaking book *Bowling Alone,* Harvard professor Robert Putnam introduced us to the notion of "social capital." Social capital refers to connections among individuals—social networks and the norms of reciprocity and trustworthiness that arise from them.[10] Putnam explored the changing nature of *bridging* (or inclusion) and *bonding* (or exclusion) in our culture, and its influence on isolation and connectedness, anonymity and relatedness. Putnam uses these cultural shifts to explain the overall decline in religious participation since the 1960s.[11]

The significance of Putnam's work is that it helps us understand how we've changed in our balance of intimacy and anonymity within organizational settings. One of the reasons that larger congregations are growing at a faster rate than smaller congregations is because of their unique capacity for accommodating both intimacy and anonymity. The large church provides an arena in which a person seeking to be unknown can be present and participate in worship and education without compromising anonymity.

Larger congregations can also meet the intimacy needs of individuals through small-group educational, service, and programming venues, where people can know and be known in deeply connectional ways. Within the large church community the same person can balance competing needs for both intimacy and isolation by choosing where and when to place herself at any given moment. People who are seeking engagement at opposite ends of the intimacy/anonymity continuum can sit comfortably side by side in the large church.

Similarly, individuals who have become overly active and engaged in the life of the congregation (to the point of burnout) can use the size and space of the large church to create pockets of anonymity where they can restore their energies and get ready to once again step into more active leadership. In other words, people can find places to hide or engage in the large church, to more effectively negotiate their own forms of involvement.

Presence of Diversity

It has often been argued that 11:00 on Sunday morning is the most segregated hour of the week in the United States. The most recent National Congregations Study indicates an increase in the racial and ethnic diversity of people in our worship services. Mark Chaves argues that the church is lagging behind other institutions in becoming more diverse. However, predominantly white congregations are becoming less white. In the period between 1998 and 2006-07:

- The percent of congregations with more than 80 percent white participation dropped from 72 to 63 percent.
- The percent of people who attend congregations in which more than 80 percent of participants are white and non-Hispanic dropped from 72 to 66 percent.
- The percent of attendees in predominantly white congregations with at least *some* Hispanic participants increased from 57 to 64 percent.
- The percent of attendees in predominantly white congregations with at least *some* recent immigrants bumped up from 39 to 51 percent.

- The percent of attendees in predominantly white congregations with at least *some* Asian participants increased from 41 to 50 percent.[12]

The large congregation, by virtue of its size, is better equipped than the smaller congregation to embrace and manage all forms of diversity (assuming that the large congregation wants to engage diversity). Multiple worship venues allow the large congregation to tailor music and worship choices that appeal to dramatically different demographic groupings. Staff team size is large enough to model the level of diversity within the congregation.

In addition to being better able to serve diverse needs, the large congregation allows members and participants to engage diversity, in measured doses, as they feel comfortable. In a small congregation when diversity shows up in the form of a visitor who presents some form of "otherness," the congregation as a whole must encounter the difference if the visitor is to feel welcome. What happens in the typical smaller church is that one or two brave souls reach out to the "different" visitor while almost everyone else tries to ignore the difference. It doesn't take long for the different person to figure out that his otherness makes people uncomfortable. He doesn't return.

The large church has the capacity to tolerate more expressions of difference. People can find their way toward others with whom they identify, without the entire congregation having to negotiate difference all of the time. Those who are uncomfortable with difference can avoid it by choosing to place distance between themselves and the one who is "other." And those who embrace diversity can find meaningful expressions of the differences they seek. Congregants balance the tension between engaging differences when it feels safe and retreating to more homogeneous groupings when it feels right, in much the same way that they negotiate intimacy and anonymity.

Having made this argument, it must be acknowledged that some very large congregations are more homogeneous than the smallest of congregations. A congregation's capacity for embracing diversity has more to do with congregational culture and values than with size. However, given two congregations that equally embrace a culture and values that support diversity, the larger church will have a natural advantage in managing the complexities inherent in diversity.

Capacity to Make a Difference

"Think global, act local" has become a mantra in our culture. We are becoming increasingly aware of our own insignificance in the global scheme of things, and we crave ways to make a difference in our own lives and in the lives of others. Large congregations offer members and constituents the opportunity to participate in something that feels significant. A member who affiliates with a large congregation can bring her resources and her giftedness to bear on the larger whole, regardless of how small those resources might be.

The large congregation is often the first responder when a community emergency arises, because it has the organizational resources to do so. The size and prestige of the institution create a voice and platform that others pay attention to on important social issues. A small congregation can take a stand on an issue and be easily overlooked. The large congregation, by virtue of its size and status, is often a force that must be reckoned with when its leaders decide to speak out. People who struggle with a sense of insignificance in life may be drawn to a large congregation so that they can finally be part of something that makes an impact. People who are movers and shakers in their communities may similarly be drawn to these institutions, because they expect to invest themselves in places where voice matters.

THE LIMITATIONS OF LARGE

With all of the natural advantages that the large church brings to bear on our culture, it would seem evident that the large congregation has become a poster child for the future of the church. However, the large church also faces formidable challenges that may limit its capacity to serve the very culture to which it appeals.

Communication Problems

If you ask any large church leader to name the top three organizational challenges facing him or her, the topic of communication will make the list. The larger a congregation grows, the more difficult it becomes to make sure that the right and left hands of the congregation are aware of one another and informed about mutual activity. Increased size means increased complexity, and the greater the organizational complexity the harder it is to ensure that everyone has access to the same information.

In *Churchmorph,* Fuller Theological Seminary professor Eddie Gibbs talks about five megatrends influencing the churches of the West. One of those trends is the movement from the Industrial Age to the Information Age. The exponential spread of the Internet and development of powerful search engines has led to the democratization of knowledge. More uniform access to information and knowledge separates influence from control in newer organizational structures. In younger organizations (those founded since the dawn of the information age), power and the control of information and knowledge don't reside in designated authorities, but are carried in the networking of relationships. Ideas emerge from everywhere in the congregation, rather than only from the center or from the top down.[13]

Hierarchical structures that have been created to control communication and decision making will not easily adapt to life in the information age. Many large congregations are set up with just such structures. To remain relevant, large congregations must learn to function through smaller, discrete organizational subunits that allow for more equal access to information and a shared ability to innovate.

Resistance to Change

In the blockbuster movie *Titanic,* director James Cameron builds a suspense-filled scene as the ocean liner approaches the silently menacing iceberg. The audience knows that the iceberg is there; they can see its immense form looming on the horizon. The ship's captain frantically sends out orders to turn the ship in a last ditch effort to avoid a collision. The intense drama of the scene is palpable because everyone watching the film understands one fundamental principle: You can't turn an ocean liner on a dime. The *Titanic* couldn't turn quickly enough, and the rest, as they say, is history.

The large church is often compared metaphorically to an ocean liner. You can't start, stop, or turn it easily. The complexity of the large church means that it is not easily jumpstarted, it is not easily stopped when it does have momentum, and mid-stream course corrections are not accomplished without considerable effort.

The organizational structures of most of our large historic churches were designed for a different cultural context. In the context of modernity, change was more predictable and occurred at a slower pace. Today, we live in a postmodern culture of discontinuous and often unpredictable change. When new threats appear on the horizon and new opportunities present themselves, the church needs organizational structures that are flexible and adaptable. Chains of decision-making command and control get in the way in times of rapid change. Because large congregations are not generally nimble, they are not well equipped to handle the changes that the shift from modernity to postmodernity is requiring.

Continual Staff and Leadership Transition

One of the unique features of the large church is the central role of the staff team as the organizing communication and decision-making body of the church. (We'll talk more about that role in chapter 5.) The effectiveness of the large church is dependent upon a high functioning, strategically aligned team of clergy, and program and support staff. The stability of that team is critical. If the team is in conflict or turmoil, the congregation is likely to be in conflict and turmoil.

We know from the principles of team formation that every time a member of a group changes (through a new hire, termination, or departure), the team once again becomes a new team. All team members must tend to the difficult work of re-forming and norming before the collective group can once again become a high functioning team. Therefore, it behooves the large church to have a staff team that is long-tenured and stable.

However, the very nature of the staff team in the large church is that it is continually in a state of transition. Large church pastors bemoan the fact that there is always a position open on the team and always a search committee in process. Heads of staff are continually on the lookout for available new talent. Some senior clergy have developed a practice of hiring new talent when they can find it and worrying about crafting the appropriate role for the new hire after the fact (a practice of which I am not particularly fond). They know that good talent is hard to come by and that the inevitability of staff transitions will open a meaningful spot for good talent down the road.

Undercapitalization

I recently spoke with the senior pastor of a congregation that has an average weekly worshiping community of 850 people. He described his role in the congregation primarily as "venture capitalist." Venture capital (in a church) is the start-up money raised in the early stages of a high-potential growth ministry that will eventually fund itself. Pastors of large congregations are continually trying to figure out how to raise money to support the growth initiatives of the church without robbing the operating budget needed to sustain payroll and existing ministries.

I've already talked a great deal in this chapter about the relative wealth of the large church. Most pastors of large congregations, even those in the wealthiest of communities, would probably laugh at the characterization of their operating budgets as "rich." The large congregation almost never has enough money to fulfill its own dreams for mission and service. Our culture demands lots of choice and relevance in both worship and programming. This requires a continual introduction of things that feel new and fresh. That also necessitates venture capital funding to resource those start-up ministries until they become self-funding.

Large churches often have great difficulty creating a sense of urgency around fundraising and capital campaigns. The large church naturally projects an image of abundance. It is difficult to convince people that the church has any genuine need or that their financial contributions make a difference. The situation is exacerbated when the congregation operates with a sizable endowment. The average person sitting in the pew may operate with the assumption that others with far more resources are adequately providing the needed funds or that the endowment can handle it.

Lack of Alignment

The "success" of the large church today is the very thing that most threatens its future effectiveness. As growth occurs, coordinating and aligning the ministries of the church becomes more challenging. When the staff team no longer fits comfortably around a single decision-making table, the church begins to lose its sense of strategic focus. Successful ministries begin competing with one another, not just for budget dollars, but for voice in shaping decision making. Highly talented staff members compete for limited resources. They may develop fiefdoms among their loyal followers, and those followers may or may not be in sync with the larger strategic agenda set by the senior minister. Lay leaders begin to feel that they've lost their place in the decision-making life of the church as the role of staff becomes more central. The emergence of multiple good ideas, and the proliferation of programs that all have the capacity to be great, forces decision making about which good ideas to say no to. In short, keeping the entire structure aligned and focused is one of the greatest challenges in the large church and also a key to its effectiveness. In many ways the rest of this book is about mastering the challenge of alignment.

If you are reading this book, there is some aspect of the large church that speaks to you. Perhaps you have been a leader in a large church for some time and have intuitively learned about many of the things that this book will discuss. You are simply looking for language to describe what you have already learned. Perhaps you are thinking about stepping into leadership or employment in a large church for the first time, and you would like to learn more about the nature of the beast. Perhaps you are a denominational executive who struggles to understand the unique demands of the large church so that you can better relate to that part of your constituency. Regardless of what draws you into this dialogue, I invite you to examine your own presuppositions and assumptions about church size. In the chapters ahead you will have an opportunity to go deeper into five leadership systems that make the large church unique. In preparation for that journey, I invite you to pause and reflect upon your own congregational background and the various ways in which your assumptions about the rightsized congregation have been shaped by your experience.

QUESTIONS FOR INDIVIDUAL OR GROUP REFLECTION

1. What draws you toward a book focused on the leadership systems of the large church? What do you hope to gain by better understanding the workings of the large church?

2. What size congregation did you belong to when you came of age spiritually (if you were part of a church during that experience)? In what ways have your impressions about the "right way to run a church" been informed by your experience in that congregation?

3. Which attractions of the large church mentioned in this chapter personally appeal to you? Place a checkmark next to all that apply:
   - Capacity for excellence
   - Reputation for high quality
   - Broad range of choice
   - Effective use of technology
   - Space for both anonymity and intimacy
   - Presence of diversity
   - Capacity to make a difference

Are there other important advantages to you of being part of a large congregation? If so, what are those?

4. Which limitations of being in a large congregation have been personally problematic for you?
   • Communication problems
   • Resistance to change
   • Continual staff or leadership transition
   • Undercapitalization
   • Lack of alignment

Are there other limitations, not identified in this chapter, that are inherent to the large congregation experience? If so, what are they?

CHAPTER 2

How Size Changes Things

PASTOR STEVE SAT BACK IN HIS CHAIR AND SIGHED. HE HAD BEEN SERVING Trinity as head of staff for eight months and still felt like he was slogging through mud, trying to figure out his role, his relationship to the staff team and the board, and how he was supposed to focus his time and energy. This morning's staff meeting had been another exercise in frustration. He tried to lead the meeting with a firm hand, but somehow it got away from him again and turned into an exercise of competition for time and attention. Things at Trinity just didn't work the way they did in his previous congregation.

Steve thought longingly about the good people back at his previous congregation. He loved serving as head of staff in his last assignment, and he hadn't been particularly interested in leaving, but Trinity had actively recruited him to be their next leader. Now he was wondering if he'd made the biggest mistake of his vocational career in accepting the call to serve Trinity.

Steve's last assignment was a congregation with an average weekend worshiping community of 550 active worshipers. It was a large church with multiple clergy leaders and three different worship venues. He felt comfortable calling himself a large church pastor and didn't imagine that moving to a congregation with 900 people in average worship attendance would be a remarkably different leadership experience. Now he felt incredibly naïve for having made that assumption.

All of the other clergy leaders at Trinity had been on staff for at least five years. They operated effectively in their areas of specialty and didn't really seem to need or want his leadership. Similarly, members of this board had remarkable strategic clarity about what they sought to accomplish and lots of energy and opinions about how to get there. Steve hadn't been able to figure out how to make his voice count anywhere outside of the pulpit. He knew that he was supposed to concentrate on delivering relevant and polished sermons. He was feeling pretty comfortable in his worship leadership role. But beyond that, he couldn't get a read on how he should be tapping into and using his leadership influence elsewhere.

In his previous congregation the whole congregation seemed to respond easily to his touch. He was at the center of all the action. What was going on here? Had he stepped into a different operating culture when he moved across state lines to accept this position, or was there something in the dynamic of leading a congregation with 350 more people in worship that had profoundly changed everything? Was he failing?

BASIC BUILDING BLOCKS OF CONGREGATIONS

Every church, regardless of its size, is organized to accommodate different types and sizes of groups that exist to make decisions about the life of the church, provide member support and care, foster discipleship, facilitate worship, and engage in service. No church, even the very smallest of congregations, involves every member in every activity of the congregation. Consequently, some type of social architecture is needed to tend the formation and coordination of the clusters. A structure is required to orchestrate communication, relationship building, and decision making, so that the various clusters are interacting with one another in a way that allows the congregation to engage its membership and serve its mission.

In order to fully explore the complexity of large congregations, we need to first understand the basic building blocks of congregations as social organizations. People do not participate in the life of the congregation as discrete individuals. They participate in the life of the congregation through their social engagement with one another through groups.

The concept of organizational building blocks is not a new idea. The presence of organizational design, using smaller groups as building blocks, is evident in some of our earliest scriptures. In Exodus 18, we encounter an exhausted Moses who has been attempting to lead the people of Israel by managing them as one large group. He is trying to maintain one-on-one leadership relationships with each of them. Moses accepts this sage advice from his father-in-law, Jethro. "Keep a sharp eye out for competent men—men who fear God, men of integrity, men who are incorruptible—and appoint them as leaders over groups organized by the thousand, by the hundred, by fifty, and by ten" (Exod. 18:21, *The Message*).

Jethro wisely understood that the organization of the people had to include fundamental divisions into small, mid-sized and large sub-groups that would be clustered meaningfully to form the whole. But what sized groups were right for what types of activity? And how, exactly, did the various groups come together to form the whole? Scripture doesn't provide an answer to this question that can be easily transferred to congregational life today. Still, modern day pastors long for a "Jethro" to show up and make meaning out of the organizational dynamics of their congregations.

In 1993 social anthropologist Robin Dunbar wrote a groundbreaking paper on research related to group size and group limits. His work revealed that the capacity of the human brain is a key determinant in the size of the groups that we form to organize ourselves and get things done. Various sized groups tend to different types of social interaction and, therefore, serve alternative functions.

Dunbar argued that the stability of organizations and social groups is based on the intimate knowledge that individuals within a group have of one another, and their ability to use this knowledge to manage relationships. Attempts to increase any group size beyond its effective limit, which is determined by the capacity of group members to track social interaction, will inevitably result in reduced social stability, and ultimately, group fission.[1]

Humans are known to have a cognitive upper limit to the average number of individuals with whom they can form coherent personal relationships. That limit, known as the Dunbar Effect, is around 150 people. Having enough memory space to remember people's names and faces is not enough to manage 150 relationships. Group members must integrate and manage information about the constantly changing relationships among individuals within a group. Recognizing that 150 is our outer relationship limit, sociologists have been able to identify a series of smaller social building blocks that help to explain how we function in organizations with more than 150 members.

   Theodore W. Johnson, an Episcopal priest and congregational consultant, worked within the Dunbar Effect to name three basic building blocks in congregational life (the care and support group, the family group or clan, and the community group).[2] In Figure 2.1, I have adapted these three building blocks and added a fourth, the decision-making group, to explain the organizational dynamics of the large congregation.

Figure 2.1   Outer Group Effectiveness Limits

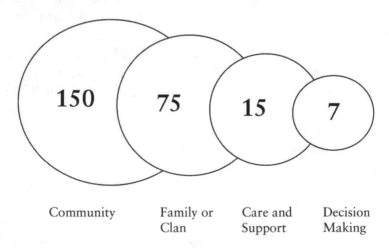

| Community | Family or Clan | Care and Support | Decision Making |

The Decision-Making Group

All parts of the congregation need to make decisions, and decisions can be made in any size group. However, larger groups have difficulty making decisions effectively. Let's explore what makes this true. A group that is trying to make a decision faces two key challenges. The first challenge is managing communication. The second is making effective decisions. Generally, including more people in a group will increase the likelihood that someone will have the information needed to make the decision and someone will propose a correct choice or solution (decision-making accuracy). However, more people produce more opinions that have to be communicated and discussed. This makes the management of communication more difficult and ends up reducing decision-making effectiveness overall. In fact, if the group is too large, the best ideas may never be heard by the group!

The difficulty of managing communication within a small group is roughly proportional to the number of possible social interactions within the group. With two people, there is only one possible social interaction. Most of us will readily acknowledge that managing even one social interaction is fraught with complexity. With three people, there are three possible two-person interactions and one three-way interaction, for a total of four possible interactions. In a four-person group, there are six possible two-way, four possible three-way, and one possible four-way interactions, for a total of eleven interactions that need to be managed.

The number of possible social interactions begins to explode in groups with more than five people. Large groups require skillful leadership and formal structures in order to function effectively. Formal structures such as parliamentary procedures work by deliberately stifling many of the possible social interactions. Unfortunately, reducing interaction can also stifle creativity and ensure that most decision making will be dominated by the most politically influential individuals in the room, whether or not they have the best ideas.[3]

The ideal decision-making unit is five people. A group of five can often work easily with a consensus model of decision making. Five is also an odd number, which prevents tie votes in majority-rule decision making. Additional group members do not greatly improve the quality of decisions made, but they significantly increase group management problems. Although not optimal, working groups of seven can still make high-quality decisions. The number of interactions that must be managed is significantly more than in a group of five but still manageable. The additional two bodies in the group can add energy, diversity of thought, and extra hands to carry out the work of the group. Working with more than seven group members exponentially increases the number of social interactions into the hundreds, making it truly impossible for group members to engage each person and every idea.

In the very large congregation the decision-making group of five to seven most prominently shows up in the form of executive decision-making bodies within the staff team or governing board, or as a bridge between the staff team and the governing board. These groups are often regarded with high levels of suspicion. People may refer to the group as the kitchen cabinet or as the pastor's *inside* group. Large church leaders often ask me if it's unhealthy for a congregation to have this inside group of leaders, which seems to be making some of the important decisions. Depending upon the emotional health of group members, their skills in decision making, and their openness to input from other groups, my response is typically to affirm their existence. Large churches need these smaller decision-making units, housed within larger working groups, to maintain a strategic focus in their decision making.

We also see the decision-making limit of seven played out within staff team dynamics. As a staff team grows in size, it must continually reorganize itself into meaningful decision-making bodies of five to seven people in order to work effectively. Thus we encounter the emergence of specialty sub-teams within the larger staff team (e.g., the program directors group, the admin staff, the children's ministry staff, the pastoral care team, etc.) When the team is not organized into smaller decision-making bodies, the work of the group changes to accommodate what the group is capable of doing. When the group becomes too large, their gatherings turn away from decision making and towards reporting, support, and care. The group creates an agenda for the type of work that it can effectively accomplish together. The head of staff may long for a group that does more decision making and become frustrated when the group continually reverts to communication, care, and support mode . . . not recognizing that this is happening because the group is too large.

The Care-and-Support Group

The foundational *social* grouping for human beings consists of a small group of between 9 and 25 individuals, referred to by sociologists as a "sympathy group." This group consists of the individuals with whom one has special ties and maintains regular contact. These are the relationships that provide us with the greatest intimacy, mutual support, and care. In the world of congregations, these groups are embodied in our small group ministries, smaller Sunday school classes, and ministry teams. These sympathy groups are often homogeneous in nature and often represent the people we turn to in our deepest moments of need.

The outer effectiveness limit of a sympathy group is based upon the human capacity to manage social grooming, forms of personal contact that produce group cohesion. Anecdotally, group members report how increasingly difficult it becomes to maintain the effectiveness of a sympathy group once the group number exceeds 12 members. The tension of the outer limit in these groups is most painfully felt between 12 and 15 members. Once the group exceeds 12 members, social interactions need to change in order to maintain group cohesion. In a group that exceeds 15 members, people begin reporting that they don't get their fair share of time, and some members begin to recede into the background. Attendance becomes lax because people don't feel personally valued. Trust becomes difficult because individuals begin to lose track of one another and have too much difficulty managing all of the possible relationships.

One of three things typically happens when a sympathy group passes the 15-member mark. Most commonly the group naturally shrinks back to a more manageable number, because people are unhappy with the group dynamics and abandon it. Sometimes the group has the clarity that it needs to split into two groups, which restores the ability of the group to offer support and care, and two new effective sympathy groups are formed. Finally, some sympathy groups, by expending lots of organized energy around communication, continue to grow through the 15-person threshold limit and become clan or family-sized groups (see the next category).

In the organizational dynamics of the large church, we often see the outer limit of the care-and-support group come into play in the management structure that supports small group ministries. Small groups are continually growing, splitting, or declining in response to the outer effectiveness limits of living, breathing groups. A pastor of discipleship may find that she can manage 8 to 10 care and support groups. She can keep track of the leaders, coach them in their development, and assist with the selection of curriculum. However, when those groups grow in membership and bump up against the effective limit for care and support, some of the groups split, and the pastor suddenly finds she is overseeing fifteen groups. She can no longer provide effective leadership. The group leaders begin to feel isolated and unsupported. An organizational restructuring is required to introduce another level of leadership, to coach the leaders of these groups, and to keep the collective network of care and support in place.

The Clan or Family Group

The next building block in organizational structure is the group of 25 to 75 individuals, which might be thought of as the clan or family group. This group is much less homogenous than the care and support group and may be intergenerational. In large congregations we often see the clan or family group at work in larger Sunday school classes, choirs, youth groups, and men's and women's ministry groups.

Groups of this size are generally thought of as nonexclusive groups, meaning that they are not the only group in which an individual participant is involved. The clan is too large to offer individual care and support to every member of the group, so most people within the group also belong to a sympathy group in some other part of the congregation, or within the larger family group. So, for example, while the Sunday evening gathering of the full youth group operates like a clan system, a member also meets on Wednesday nights with his small support group of youth, a subset of the youth ministry program.

The governance of clan groups is family-style leadership, with the most respected people serving as leaders (the choir director, the Sunday school superintendent, the youth group advisor). Member roles, rights, and privileges are determined by respect and position. The outer threshold limit of clan groups is around 50. Beyond this number the family support structure begins to disintegrate.

We witness the organizational structure of a congregation shifting when a ministry group hits about 50 or 60 members. Consider a thriving youth ministry that grows to include 60 student participants and suddenly finds it can no longer operate effectively with its existing structure. Participants begin reporting that their needs and preferences aren't being met. Leaders report that they can't keep track of the kids. The ministry begins to falter. Leaders decide that the senior high and junior high youth ministries must be split into two different groups or clans. Structurally, some changes need to be made. The existing youth director either needs to be appointed as the overseer of the entire program, with the appointment of new senior high and junior high leaders (which adds a layer of leadership structure), or the existing youth director assumes leadership of one of the two new groups and a new director is hired to provide leadership for the other group, which maintains the current organizational structure but adds one more direct report to whomever is supervising youth ministries.

An equally palpable phenomenon occurs when a clan group shrinks in size. Recently, I worked with a congregation that has experienced a significant decline in membership. Once upon a time they had a large youth ministry with 75 active members and separate middle school and high school ministries. Today, there are only 12 kids in the middle school youth program and 13 kids in the senior high youth program. Leaders have been adamant about keeping the two programs separate, because they are convinced that they need independent programs to maintain program excellence and attract new members.

In fact, the students are clamoring for combining the two programs for certain activities, because they want to belong to a social grouping that feels larger and more vibrant, one that provides stronger social identity. They want to belong to a clan. The congregation's insistence on maintaining separate groups has produced two care-and-support groups that have a decidedly different feel from what one large clan would have.

The Community Group

Once a group has exceeded 75 participants, it is no longer capable of maintaining itself as a clan system and, if it survives, the group must become a community group. The community group is primarily a fellowship group. It corresponds to a typical village unit in pre-modern history. It provides a broad group identity for its participants and some sense of belonging and safety. It does not provide the membership identity or privileges of the clan-sized group nor the care and support system of the sympathy-sized group. The principal leaders of the community are often elected or appointed and serve by legitimate consent. This is the group that represents Dunbar's outer limit of social functioning. Community groups can function with between 50 and 150 members. However, growing to 150 requires very effective group facilitation and lots of time spent by the group in social grooming.

The community group, as a building block of organizational structure, may be more prevalent in the medium-sized congregation than it is in the very large congregation. A pastoral-sized church, taken as a whole, is a stand-alone community group. A program-sized congregation is a congregation that is managed as an amalgam of small, family, and community groups, with the community groups represented by the worshiping communities.

In some large congregations the individual worshiping communities function as community groups, so long as the worshiping community does not exceed 150 participants. Most worshiping communities in large congregations exceed this size, however, and the gathered worshippers don't really function as a singular group. They may identify themselves by their style of worship and the time they gather ("I attend the 9:00 a.m. contemporary service in fellowship hall"), but they don't constitute a truly interactive social group. Participants are accustomed to the fact that they don't know all the other worshipers in the room.

Churches that are in decline may experience organizational stress when groups that once functioned in the 75 to 150 range are no longer large enough to constitute a community. Consider a congregation that offers a small Sunday morning worship service at an early hour to accommodate some of its senior members. When the worship service first began, average attendance was around 125. Recently, through various kinds of attrition, the size of that community has dropped below 75 members, and the group has begun to feel out of sorts in its worship space. It wants to feel like its own community, but in fact the group dynamics are functioning more like a clan. The clan nature of the gathering has become ingrown and is inhibiting the welcome of new worshipers. Church leaders are facing the painful reality that they need to combine this group with another worship group in order to maintain a vibrant worshiping community.

One place that the community-sized group regularly expresses itself in the large congregation is at the all-church meeting. Anytime the full congregation is called together for decision making, a community-sized group tends to show up. This seems to hold true regardless of the size of the congregation. Whether the congregation draws 500 or 2,000 people together in average weekend attendance, the number of people who will show up for an open congregational meeting is typically 75 to 150 people, a community sized group.

Another place in the large church where the outer community limit of 150 expresses itself is in the assignment of staff team responsibilities. A long-standing practice of staff team design suggests that one program staff employee is needed to support the programming needs of every 150 people in average worship attendance. Many large congregations seek to manage the collective whole by having each clergy or program staff member keep track of his or her own 150-member community. This works well in some size categories, but not others. We'll discuss the validity of this staff team design principle further in chapter 5.

PUTTING THE BUILDING BLOCKS TOGETHER

The large congregation is a complex blend of decision-making groups, care-and-support groups, clan groups, and communities all loosely orchestrated by the governing board and staff team. The configuration of groups is in constant motion as groups form and reform in response to their outer limits of effectiveness. Day-to-day the leaders of the congregation are not particularly aware of or distracted by the organization and re-organization of groups. In the large church, groups are forming, reforming, and dissolving all the time.

What is noteworthy are the moments when the configuration of groups, clans, and communities in the congregation place stress upon the organizational structure of the church, such that the structure is stretched beyond its capacity. Suddenly, the senior pastor becomes aware of his level of exhaustion. He just can't seem to keep up with the incessant needs of the staff team and congregants. The staff team seems disoriented in staff meetings and can't seem to accomplish what it needs to do in the staff-meeting format that has always worked before. The governing board seems to lose its focus and finds itself getting distracted by management issues that should be handled by the staff team. In other words, the structure that once worked suddenly stops working effectively, and leaders find that they are investing far too much energy into the management of complexity. What has happened?

There are five basic leadership systems in the congregation that collectively manage the complexity of the organization. These five systems are highly interdependent. When change occurs in one of these systems, it tends to produce change in the other systems. These systems include:

1. Clergy Leadership Roles
2. Staff Team Design and Function
3. Governance and Board Function
4. Acculturation and Leadership of the Laity
5. Forming and Executing Strategy

These five leadership systems are in constant motion in the large congregation. As the social structure of the congregation adapts itself to daily changes in group function, these systems tend to remain largely stable. Leaders come and go, policies are formed and adapted, groups form and dissolve, but the basic interaction of the five systems remains relatively constant.

However, just as the basic building blocks of the congregation have their particular outer limits, so leadership systems have their outer limits. A senior clergyperson assumes a particular leadership role and style that is highly effective in a church with weekend worship attendance of 700. The clergyperson is surprised to discover that the leadership role begins losing its effectiveness when the church adds an additional worship service and now hosts 850 in weekend worship. Or, a staff team that was humming along downsizes by two program leaders in response to declining attendance, and suddenly the dynamics of the team are thrown off. The staff team maintains some momentum but notices how much more energy it suddenly takes to function well as a team.

When one of these five leadership systems begins to experience stress, the tension is often transferred to the other four leadership systems. One part of the leadership system may begin to adapt in response to increased complexity in the congregation, but other leadership systems lag behind. This produces strain on the collective whole.

One of the remarkable things about these five leadership systems is that they tend to reach their outer limits at predictable moments, based on worship attendance or budget size. We often refer to the period of time that a congregations approaches and moves through these limits as a transition zone. Some refer to transition zones as "attendance ceilings," because they observe a congregation's weekend attendance repeatedly climbs to a predictable level and then drops back down. When a congregation hits one of these transition zones, it must intentionally adapt all of the five leadership systems, or the congregation won't be able to accommodate the added complexity. The systems have reached their effectiveness limits and cannot accommodate additional people or groups without being redesigned.

In the next chapter we'll talk more about where the critical transition zones seem to occur in large congregations, and we'll explore the unique dynamics of each system in each zone. For now, let's work on developing a clearer understanding of the five systems themselves and how they tend to adapt themselves in different size ranges.

FIVE SYSTEMS IN MOTION

There are probably an infinite number of ways to label the systems of a congregation. Each time that I speak about these five systems, I am challenged by someone who can name an alternative set of systems that also change and morph in response to the size dynamics of the congregation. I will not argue that these five systems make up the definitive structure in any congregation. However, I have found through my consulting practice that when I invite congregations to focus on adapting these five systems in tandem, they seem to report considerable relief from their organizational sense of being "stuck." These may not be the only or definitive five leadership systems of the church, but they are five systems that matter.

Clergy Leadership Roles

People have long understood that clergy need a unique set of leadership skills to function well as head of staff in the large church. However, across the spectrum of large congregations, clergy face different kinds of leadership challenges and must shape their roles accordingly. One size doesn't fit all when it comes to large church leadership.

At the lower end of the large church spectrum (400-800 in attendance), the head of staff has to let go of a purely relationship style of leadership and engage the congregation from a more managerial perspective. Higher in the size range (800-1,200 in attendance), the head of staff needs to become less managerial and more strategic in her leadership.

Assistant clergy roles are also very different in these two size ranges. The congregation that has just become large enough to hire an associate pastor hires a generalist. In this congregation the associate is responsible for ministering to the whole congregation, in much the same way that the senior minister does. Although he may have a specific portfolio unique to his role (e.g., religious education), his job is also to function as backup to the senior minister, stepping in when the senior is unavailable. The associate in this sized congregation is often on a pass-through trajectory, engaging this role for a brief period of time before moving on to get his "own" congregation.

In the larger church, the portfolio of the associate is often a reflection of a unique vocational calling. The associate functions as a called specialist in a particular area of ministry (e.g., spiritual formation) and does not view the role as a pass-through assignment. He is not a backup to the senior minister but a professional leader of the church with a clearly defined role with firm boundaries.

Clergy skill sets and the leadership styles in different sized large congregations will be explored more fully in chapter 4.

Staff Team Design and Function

In a congregation with an average weekend worshiping community of 400, the staff team structure is flat. Every member of the staff team reports directly to the head of staff. When the staff team gathers, the meeting structure is fairly straightforward. Key members of the team can function together as a single decision-making body. Everyone sits around the table together to manage the daily life of the congregation.

A congregation with 1,000 weekly worship participants is a much different beast. Multiple supervisory levels exist. Some members of the staff team have two reporting levels between themselves and the senior minister. The entire staff team meets together only occasionally, for very brief periods of time, for updates by the head of staff. Every member of the team belongs to a smaller sub-unit of the staff team (e.g., the worship team, the pastoral care team, the children's ministry team, and so forth). These smaller sub-units of the staff team have their own team meetings, and the collective strategic alignment of the whole staff team is orchestrated through a carefully crafted set of agendas for each sub-team meeting.

The structure, design, and function of staff teams in various sized large congregations will be explored further in chapter 5.

Governance and Board Function

The governing body in a congregation with 400 in weekly worship is likely to be a board that contributes a lot of hands-on support to the staff team in the day-to-day management of the congregation. This governing board is preoccupied with trying to grow the budget in order to hire more staff that it desperately needs, while tending to the development of lay leaders. There is never adequate leadership to give life to the dreams of the congregation. Most of the leaders that serve on this board are chosen for their ability to represent the collective thinking of the congregation.

A congregation with 1,000 in weekly worship functions with a very different kind of board. This board has fully delegated the daily management of the church to the staff team. It focuses on the overall leadership strategy of the congregation and on creating accountability systems so that the congregation lives into its vision. The board is probably smaller in number than the governing board in the church of 400, and the people who serve on the board possess demonstrated expertise as strategic leaders in other kinds of organizations. They are selected to serve on the board because of their leadership capacity, not because they represent specific interest groups of the congregation.

The design and function of governing boards in different sized large congregations will be further explored in chapter 6.

Membership Acculturation

Membership acculturation is a challenge in any sized congregation. But different sizes of large congregations must manage the process of acculturation in different ways. The largest obstacle to acculturation in a congregation with 400 in worship is trying to imagine and organize new programming and worship venues that will attract larger numbers of people to the congregation. Once people become regular participants in worship, the road-map for their assimilation into the life of the church becomes apparent to them and others around them. They will be invited to join a Sunday school class or small group that will become their support-and-care group and the rest will unfold from there. The acculturation process is largely managed through the clergy staff who, through personal contact, collectively keep track of the entire congregation.

In a congregation with 1,000 in worship, the venues for entry into the life of the congregation are significantly more complex than they are in the church of 400. There are so many possible points of entry and so many ways that people can think of themselves as active participants (through affiliation with the school, by engaging in social justice programming, through family affiliation with the youth ministry program, and so forth) that people can't be easily tracked. The collective clergy team can no longer keep track of everyone, and a full-time director of membership is hired. This person's job is not to personally track newcomers, but to create a seamless system of acculturation for newcomers and to create a more comprehensive data bank of information about the membership of the congregation. In this size congregation, new people are acculturated through a carefully constructed series of entry points, classes, and groups on their way to becoming fully engaged leaders in the congregation.

A more complete discussion of acculturation challenges and the organizational structures that address them will be undertaken in chapter 7.

Strategy Formation and Execution

In every sized congregation, it is the responsibility of the governing board to formulate the strategic direction of the congregation with the involvement of the congregation and the input of the staff team. Furthermore, it is the function of the board to define the policies that will empower the staff team to manage and execute the strategy that has been defined. Having established that common ground, the way in which growth and strategy are actually formed and executed varies considerably with the size of the congregation. (Note: "growth" as the term is used here doesn't necessarily refer to numerical growth. It might represent growth in spiritual formation, growth in programming, growth in community outreach, and so forth.)

In a congregation with average attendance of 400, the congregation itself must come together to agree upon strategy and growth objectives. The congregation is still working through its ambivalence about being large. A singular vision of the church and its strategy may not yet exist.

In a congregation with 1,000 in weekly attendance, the need for growth is assumed, and it is being managed in multiple places in the congregation at the same time. The biggest strategic challenge in a congregation of this size is the issue of alignment. How does the left hand know what the right hand is doing? How does the senior minister lead in such a way that the focus of the staff team doesn't drift? How does the congregation decide which areas of church life it will pursue with excellence and passion, and which great ideas it will say no to, in service to a greater yes someplace else in the congregation?

A more complete discussion of growth and strategy will take place in chapter 8.

GETTING FROM HERE TO THERE

The above overview of how leadership systems evolve across the spectrum of sizes in large churches invites a series of questions. Which system changes first? How do the five leadership systems in a large congregation adapt and change together, so a church that is growing moves seamlessly from one kind of organizational system to another? How does a church that used to be much larger, but has suffered numerical loss, reduce the complexity of its system to more effectively manage its present size? What are the logical transition zones where everything must change, to ensure the future growth of the church is not restricted? Does leadership design its systems to serve the size congregation that it is or the size congregation that it seeks to become? Are the transition zones descriptive or prescriptive? These are the questions that the remaining chapters of this book will seek to answer, to the extent that answers can be provided.

The very fact that we can identify at least five leadership systems in motion at the same time is an indicator of the complexity of change that must be managed for effective organizational growth or downsizing to occur. In the next chapter we'll look at how the five systems behave in observable zones marked by attendance and operating budgets. These stages give birth to three new organizational labels for the large church: the professional church, the strategic church, and the matrix church.

As we engage this conversation, let's be careful not to let the assignment of labels trick us into believing that the transition points are easily identifiable or simply negotiated. I have yet to encounter a congregation with all five leadership systems perfectly aligned for its size. Congregations are living, breathing organisms. They grow, change, and evolve under our feet as we walk. Even the most insightful and well-intentioned congregations rarely operate with perfectly aligned leadership structures. However, the congregation that actively tends to the rightsizing of its leadership systems generally finds that it has more energy to devote to mission, discipleship, and service.

QUESTIONS FOR INDIVIDUAL OR GROUP REFLECTION

1. Name the key decision-making groups in your congregation, and record the size of those groups below. Are these groups appropriately sized to promote effective decision making? If not, what prevents the group from being more appropriately sized?

Group Name	Group Size
_____	_____
_____	_____
_____	_____
_____	_____
_____	_____

2. Where can you see care-and-support groups, clan-sized groups, and community-sized groups at work in your congregation? How critical is their presence to the overall social functioning of the congregation?

3. This chapter introduced the notion of "outer limits" in group dynamics. An outer limit presents itself when a group can no longer effectively function in an expected capacity, because the group has grown too large to effectively perform its assigned role. Think about the past 12 months in your own congregation, and identify those incidents or situations that might indicate a group is operating outside of its effective limit.

4. This chapter introduced five key leadership systems that stay in continual motion in the large church: clergy leadership roles, staff team design and function, governance and board structure, acculturation and the role of laity, and strategy formation and execution. Reflect on these five systems in your own congregation. Which systems seem to be functioning effectively, and which seem to be taxed beyond their limits?

CHAPTER 3

Living Large

Exploring Large Church Size Categories

RANDY IS THE PASTOR OF FELLOWSHIP COMMUNITY CHURCH. HIS CON-
gregation is 23 years old, and Randy is the only senior pastor that
the congregation has ever known. The congregation was a church
plant sponsored by his denomination. When you meet Randy, you
are immediately aware of his entrepreneurial orientation. This is
a guy who loves change and likes to stir things up. It doesn't take
long before you begin asking yourself, "How did one congregation ever manage to keep this guy as their leader for twenty-some
years?"

The answer is pretty simple. Fellowship Church grew rapidly and became a large congregation within three years of being
founded. Since then the church has managed to stay on a pretty
constant growth trajectory. Today the congregation operates on
two campuses and has a combined worshiping community of
around 1,100. Randy will be the first person to tell you that he
hasn't led one congregation for his entire career. He has actually
led four different congregations. He just didn't have to relocate
or accept a different call to have that experience. The continued
growth of Fellowship Church presented Randy with the opportunity to reinvent his leadership style and the leadership systems of
the church. It's a tribute to Randy's leadership that he was able
to demonstrate the skills needed to make all of those transitions.
Randy can tell you with great clarity when and where the key transition points took place; the moments when everything stopped
working for a while and had to be reinvented to serve the next

chapter of congregational life. Randy will tell you that leadership through a size transition is all about paying attention to the signals the systems of the congregation are sending you.

In chapter 2, I identified five leadership systems that stay in motion at all times in the large church. These include clergy leadership roles, staff team design and function, board function and governance, membership assimilation, and the formation and execution of strategy. I provided examples to illustrate how these systems behave as a church first becomes large (around 400 in worship) compared with how they behave at the largest end of the size spectrum (approaching 2,000 in worship).

This chapter will describe how the five systems evolve together, at observable and predictable points on the size continuum. We'll look for natural transition points when all five systems seem to transition in response to increased complexity. We'll also explore four natural zones where those five systems stabilize and accommodate additional complexity and growth without shifting. We'll talk about the basic organizing principle that leaders need to focus on in each of these size categories.

Before we can begin to explore the size plateaus and transition zones in the large congregation, we need to reach some common understanding about how size and complexity are measured. What is the appropriate way to talk about the size of a congregation?

MEASURING SIZE AND COMPLEXITY

Life changed in unexpected ways when my husband and I had our third child. Becoming first-time parents had been a jarring experience. We expected life as we knew it to disappear upon the arrival of that first child, and although we were stressed by the transition, we were more or less prepared for the turmoil. The arrival of the second child was almost a non-event, hardly a disruption. He fit easily into the lifestyle that we had established after the arrival of the first child, and life was humming along pretty smoothly within six weeks of his arrival. The same could not be said with the arrival of the third.

I suppose I expected some kind of economy of scale in raising children. The second child had been so easy to fold in alongside the first that I expected the arrival of the third to feel even easier. I was not prepared for the adaptations that I had to make with his arrival. Our third had a very mild-mannered temperament, so it wasn't that he was a difficult baby. It was just that having three children under the age of six required lifestyle adaptations that snuck up on me unexpectedly.

Life with three was more complex on so many levels. The vehicle that we drove wasn't big enough to hold three in the back seat, so we needed to switch over to a minivan. Much of the baby equipment we had purchased or received with number one (swings, strollers, and the like) was designed to last for only two children, so those items needed to be replaced. When my husband and I took the kids out as a family unit, we were very aware that the children now outnumbered the adults. The kids seemed to realize this as well, and they took full advantage of it. When I took them out alone, it became painfully obvious that I had only two hands, and there were three of them. Finding a time when everyone was awake to go places became difficult. Finding time when all three were asleep, so I could get things done around the house, was equally challenging. For a while, I felt like a prisoner in my own home until I adopted new processes for coping with the additional complexity caused by the third child's arrival.

This deep sense of disorientation is typical of the kind of unrest a congregation experiences when it bumps into the outer threshold limits of its leadership systems. Everything seems to be sailing along smoothly, and then suddenly, and rather arbitrarily, it all starts taking too much energy to sustain. There is loss of momentum, loss of energy, loss of efficiency, and loss of focus. The difficulty in hitting transition zones in the life of the church is that the cause of the disorientation is not immediately evident. Adapting to the increased complexity is not as easily accomplished as saying, "Well, we've just added a third child into the mix."

Understanding the capacity limits of congregational systems is *not* simply an exercise in measuring attendance. For decades now Alban has used the average number of people in weekend worship attendance (adults and children) as an indicator of the real size of a congregation. We've long understood that membership numbers are pretty meaningless indicators of size, because of how loosely membership rolls are managed, and because of how differently congregations define membership. Most congregations do some level of attendance tracking on weekends, however, and those numbers are available to help us talk about size. Furthermore, the average number of people who show up to participate in the worship life of the congregation is a pretty good indicator of the size of the active congregation, the part of the congregation that is likely to place demands on the leadership systems of the church. So, average weekend attendance is a good benchmark of the congregation's size. But many other factors also need to be taken into consideration.

Increasingly, I'm discovering that attendance numbers don't fully reflect the organizational complexity of large congregations and may not be the best indicator of church size. Other factors include:

- The size of the operating budget. Budget size shapes staffing capacity. The larger the staff team, the more programming the congregation can sustain. More programming produces greater complexity. Congregations that are able to support higher operating budgets (either because they are located in affluent areas, they have endowment funds, or they have unusually generous congregants) will demonstrate the organizational attributes of a much larger congregation than their attendance suggests.
- Affluence. Congregations that are located in affluent communities often discover that they have lower weekend attendance patterns than their less affluent counterparts. Affluent families often own vacation homes or have the means to get away on weekends, which takes them away from the worshiping life of the congregation. Although these people think of themselves as active participants in the life of the congregation, and although these people place demands on the leadership structure of the church through their

participation, and although these people contribute significantly to the operating budget, they don't show up in worship attendance figures.

- Midweek ministries. Increasingly, large congregations are offering midweek ministry opportunities. Congregants who find that they are too busy on weekends to attend worship may participate actively in the life of the congregation during the week. Their participation in midweek programming places demands on the leadership systems of the church but isn't reflected in average worship attendance.
- Building size and function. Large congregations generally operate elaborate campuses or physical plants. When these buildings are actively used throughout the week, the stress on the operating systems of the congregation is increased. Staff members must tend to the needs of the building and the needs of the people using the building. This adds to the complexity of managing the congregation without a commensurate increase in the size of the worshiping community.
- Number of worship venues and sites. A congregation with 1,000 active members who all worship in a single venue at the same time will have a much different leadership structure in place than the same sized congregation that operates with five different worship venues. The addition of each worshiping venue adds complexity to the leadership systems of the church.
- Affiliated nonprofits. Many large congregations operate 501(c)3 organizations in the form of preschools, day schools, social service organizations, family life centers, and the like. These organizations operate with their own budgets and governance structures, but their attachment to the large congregation increases the complexity of managing the church itself. Again, none of this complexity shows up in a weekend worship attendance number.

So, what is the correct way to measure the size of a congregation? There isn't an easy answer. Weekend worship attendance is at least a starting place, and for many congregations, it is the definitive measure. However, when any of the above extenuating circumstances are present, I believe that you need to let the leadership systems themselves tell you in which size category the congregation is actually functioning. What type of leadership style and focus is the senior pastor using, and does it seem to be working? How is the staff team organized? Are there multiple reporting layers and sub-teams within the larger staff team? Where is the board's focus? Based upon the leadership behavioral patterns of the church, you can begin to articulate what size the congregation really is, and from there you can figure out if all of the leadership systems of the congregation are in alignment.

In spite of all of the limitations inherent in using average worship attendance, it's probably still the most reliable indicator with which to begin the size conversation. If we have to make generalizations about where size transition zones begin and end, we might as well work with average worship attendance as anything else. The important thing for the reader to remember is that individual circumstance is more important than generalized experience. None of us can really identify the size at which an individual congregation's leadership systems hits its capacity limits. Two congregations, one with a worshiping community of 400 and one with a community of 275, may very well hit a set of capacity limits at about the same time. The critical thing to pay attention to is the alignment of systems. When stress within one of the systems begins to make itself felt, leaders must attend to shifts in the other systems as well.

The Wisdom of the Hermit Crab

A favorite book in my home as my children were growing up was Eric Carle's *A House for Hermit Crab*.[1] The book begins with Hermit Crab chafing against his shell, which has become too tight. Recognizing that he has outgrown his shell, Hermit steps out of the shell onto the ocean floor in search of a new home that will better serve his larger size. He's a bit frightened at first, recognizing how vulnerable he is after leaving his safe and familiar home behind. Before long, Hermit finds a new spacious shell to adopt as his residence. Over the course of the next year he adds an array of sea creatures to his shell, daily companions that help to adorn, clean, and protect his new home. In time, the new shell and its interdependent biological parts becomes a home every bit as comfortable as the one left behind, but more suitable to his new size. As the story draws to a close, Hermit Crab once again begins to experience the pinch of a shell that has become too small. He sets off again in search of a shell that is better equipped to hold him, leaving the carefully constructed home behind for use by a new tenant.

This simply told fable is replete with gentle messages about growing, moving on, accepting new challenges, and interdependence. It serves as a wonderful metaphor for the congregation that is thinking about adopting a new structure to appropriately accommodate its size. Congregations become accustomed to living in the systems that they have built up over time. They know how to get things done within their existing structures, even if it is cumbersome. It is scary to think about moving out of those systems into unknown territory that may prove life-threatening at first. Many congregations, preferring the safety and security of what is known, will continue to add crusty coral and anemones to structures that can no longer support their size. A moment arrives in the life of a congregation passing through size thresholds when a difficult decision must be made to adopt new leadership systems. Getting all of your leaders to acknowledge that a change must be made and to arrive at consensus about the direction of that change can be a daunting task. Let us carry the metaphor of the Hermit Crab with us as we contemplate the different leadership systems that best suit different sized congregations.

THE MULTI-CELL CHURCH
(NOT A LARGE CHURCH)

The first size category included here is actually *not* a large congregation. The multi-cell church is a medium-sized church that is looking toward becoming large. I believe it is important to begin with a description of this size category in order to develop a full understanding of the leadership challenges that congregations face in larger size categories. How things get accomplished in the multi-cell church becomes a reference point for later challenges.

Congregations will often arrive in this size category when their annual operating budget falls between $500,000 and $1,000,000 *or* when their average weekly worship attendance reaches between 250 and 400 people *or* when one or more of the factors identified in the previous section bump the church into this behavioral pattern. This is the congregation that is clearly past the critical limit of 150 relationships identified by Dunbar and discussed in chapter 2. It can no longer think of itself as a single-celled organism with a single clergy leader.

The congregation is learning to behave like a complex, multi-celled church, and the organizational challenge that drives much of its decision making and attention is leadership development. In the multi-celled church there are never enough leaders to do the work that is needed to generate consistently excellent programs. This congregation is largely guided by lay leaders, and the staff team exists to support and coordinate the laity in their ministry.

The multi-celled church has already learned some things about managing multiple cell groups. However, decisions about whether the church wants to get any larger have to be carefully examined. Growth will stagnate if the congregation does not come to terms with its identity as a complex congregation where everyone doesn't know everyone else and not everyone is cared for by the pastor. The decision to grow larger has to be resolved with the full congregation; it is not a decision that the board or staff team can make on behalf of the congregation. This size congregation is often grappling with whether it wants or needs to add multiple worship services. Even though the church has passed beyond the threshold where everyone can know everyone else, there may still be a strong desire to keep the number of relationships in the congregation intimate and manageable. If growth is an objective, the culture of the congregation must be intentionally adapted to allow for multiple congregations to reside within the same corporate body.

The assimilation challenge in the multi-celled church is about creating enough programs of excellent quality to attract a continued stream of newcomers into the life of the congregation. Many people are attracted to a multi-celled congregation, because of the emerging quantity and quality of programs offered. The congregation that fails to develop enough new leaders to provide ongoing quality programming will stagnate and falter.

The pastor in a multi-celled congregation leads primarily through vision casting. His or her principal leadership focus involves discerning and articulating an energizing vision for the congregation, one that will hold together the growing number of operating cells. The pastor must also be able to guide congregational leaders as they translate vision into action. One pastor described the challenge this way:

> The real tension exists in trying to hold the vision and in helping to build the vision with others. In this setting we have emerging multiple congregations within the larger congregation. How do you allow various groups to emerge and recognize that those communities have their own identity, but are still rooted to the larger congregation? This size congregation calls to mind the story of five blindfolded people all touching and describing different parts of an elephant. Each describes his experience of the elephant remarkably differently, and someone has to frame the larger picture so that they all understand that they are experiencing the same animal. That someone has to be me—the pastor.

The overwhelming challenge of the multi-celled church pastor is learning to communicate a caring presence to the congregation without being the "one" who provides care to each congregation member. This head of staff is learning how to focus his or her energies on other members of the staff team and key lay leaders, who in turn are providing congregational care.

Staff members in the multi-celled church are just beginning to identify themselves as a team and not as a group of individuals pursuing separate ministries. Most members of the team are still generalists, serving the needs of wide constituent groups. A few specialized staff members (for example, a children's ministry director) have been added to the team, and the team is challenged by learning to balance and honor the role of the specialist alongside the role of the generalist.

The governing board of the multi-celled church is learning to organize its work around the mission and vision of the congregation. Lay leaders are grasping the importance of saying no to ideas that distract the congregation from its mission. The board is also largely preoccupied with the development of new lay leaders to fill the growing volume of leadership needs.

THE PROFESSIONAL CHURCH

Congregations occupy another stable size plateau when they operate with an annual budget of between $1 million and $2 million *or* when weekly worship attendance reaches between 400 and 800 *or* when the congregation manifests some other unique characteristic that drives its behavior into this size zone. I refer to this size congregation as the professional church, because most of its behavior is driven by the need to professionalize operations. The congregation realizes that the church's programming has outgrown the managerial capacity of its lay leaders. Lay leaders don't have the time and energy necessary to both sustain excellence in existing programming and continually introduce new programming, so the demand for a staff team of specialists emerges. The congregation whose budget can keep pace with the need for a specialized staff will find itself crossing over and becoming a professional church. The professionalization of the church does not suggest that laity play a lesser role in the life of the congregation. It does suggest that they have to learn to play a different kind of role.

In the professional church, growth is related to capacity. In most congregations of this size, members have already embraced having multiple worship services, and they have let go of the notion that everyone will know everyone else. Ideas abound in this congregation, but they are limited by the time and energy of the staff team or the physical limitations of the facility. Consequently, the congregation's ability to grow is largely a function of the size of its budget.

Assimilation of new members in the professional church becomes as much about watching the back door as bringing people in through the front door. The professional congregation can quickly feel anonymous to newcomers, so finding innovative ways to keep track of members and to engage people beyond the Sunday worship experience takes a great deal of leadership energy.

The pastor of the professional congregation is letting go of a purely relational style of leadership and learning a more managerial style. This pastor has already learned to shift the focus of her pastoral care away from the general body and toward the board, the staff team, and key lay leaders. The pastor still maintains a strong emphasis on vision formation but is becoming equally adept at managing the performance of the congregation through careful coordination of the work of staff team and board. She is figuring out how to create and sustain the performance management cycle of the congregation through goal setting, budgeting, performance review, and a coaching leadership style.

As staff members take over many of the functions previously managed by volunteers, the staff needs to find new and creative ways to actively engage the laity in the life and ministry of the congregation. The staff is increasingly moving away from a generalist orientation (associate pastor) to a specialist orientation (pastor of senior adult ministry). An executive leadership team may emerge to coordinate and guide the work of the staff team in this size congregation. This team may consist of select staff members or a combination of both staff and lay leaders. An administrator may be appointed in this size congregation to relieve the senior pastor from having to manage the church's day-to-day financial, personnel, building maintenance, and information technology needs.

In the professional congregation, the governing board faces a significant adaptive challenge. Leaders who were once so instrumental in making all of the programs of the church happen must learn a more distant approach to leadership. The governing board in the professional church relinquishes the daily management of the church to the staff team. Working with the pastor on vision articulation, the governing board is instrumental in creating policy and systems for managing performance, maintaining accountability, and preventing vision-drift. The board spends less time on the daily fiduciary work of the congregation and more time on strategic leadership.

THE STRATEGIC CHURCH

The strategic orientation of a congregation emerges as a stabilizing presence once a congregation is operating with a budget between $2 million and $4 millions *or* maintaining average weekly attendance between 800 and 1,200 *or* demonstrating some other factor that drives its behavioral patterns into this category. This congregation requires a more intentional orientation towards strategy, growth, and alignment. As congregations grow they develop complexly layered staffing structures, board structures, and governance practices. There are so many decision-making groups at work in strategic congregations that it is easy for these groups to drift out of alignment and for tremendous energies to be wasted. For example, a staff member invents a participant tracking system only to learn that someone else on the team has already invented a similar system. The board finds out that it is trying to problem solve an issue that a committee of the church already addressed. For that reason the strategic congregation must carefully align its leadership energies.

In the strategic church, people assume that the congregation must keep growing or it will stagnate and eventually decline. Nobody talks about whether the church ought to grow; growth is assumed. The congregation owns its identity as a strategic institution and expects continued growth. The work that needs to be done to continue growth (program expansions, worship excellence, and so forth) is managed by the staff team of the church; it is not the missional focus of lay leaders. The nature and direction of growth must be continually managed and planned. The challenge of the strategic church's growth is that the congregation can excel at just about anything it focuses its energies on, but it doesn't have the resources to excel at everything. This means strategic choices must be made.

Assimilation in the strategic church must be managed as a seamless process including membership, discipleship, gift discovery, and leadership development. These are all linked through a fully formed network of classes or small groups. So many avenues of entry exist in the strategic congregation that a new member can easily get lost in a maze of choices. Intentional paths of assimilation must be created and communicated to ensure that first-time attendees eventually become members and that members eventually step into leadership roles.

The challenge of the strategic church pastor is learning to lead with a strategic orientation. One pastor of a strategic church put it this way: "Whatever I pay attention to grows. If I pay too much attention to the wrong kind of conflict, it will grow. If I don't pay enough attention to a new initiative, it won't grow. I have to be extremely careful where I focus my gaze." Similarly, the strategic church pastor must learn to say no to ideas that sound attractive but risk causing the staff team and governing board to lose their focus. The strategic church pastor is always struggling to take a step back and examine the larger organizational picture. These pastors are learning to personify the mission and vision of the congregation in everything they say and do. They will often crystallize the vision of the church into short sound bites that every member of the staff team and board begins to repeat.

The staff team in the strategic church has grown so large (often well over 25 people) that it is virtually impossible for the collective group to identify itself as a single team. Consequently, the staff team begins to form itself into identifiable and manageable sub-teams (the children's ministry team, the youth team, the administrative support team, and so forth). The challenge of the staff team in the strategic church is avoiding a silo mentality, where every sub-team operates as if it were the only or most important team. Program staff members are continually challenged to keep a relational focus in ministry as the administrative components of their jobs expand. Maintaining the right balance between program and administrative support staff becomes critical as the complexity of the congregation mushrooms. Often an executive minister is appointed in this size congregation. The program staff team reports to the executive minister, who effectively runs the day-to-day operations of the church, so the senior minister is free to focus exclusively on preaching, public speaking, and fundraising.

Counterintuitively, the larger and more complex a congregation becomes, the smaller the governing board that is needed to lead it well. In the strategic church, decision making is hampered by a board that has too many people on it and committee structures that have grown too complex to allow for nimble decision making. Strategic congregations often struggle to reduce the size of their decision-making bodies because membership doesn't believe that a small group can adequately represent the full diversity of the congregation. Members are learning to trust the decision-making authority of a smaller group. The effective governing board in the strategic church focuses on strategic decision making, keeping the church focused in response to these basic questions: Who are we? What constituency do we serve? And what is God calling us to do or become?[2] These boards exist to provide a strong support-and-accountability system to the senior minister and executive minister.

THE MATRIX CHURCH

The stabilizing orientation of the strategic church begins to break down when a congregation passes 1,200 in worship *or* when the annual operating budget moves beyond $4 million *or* when some other factor adds complexity that the system can no longer accommodate. For example, the large congregation that decides to move to a multi-site ministry model may encounter a level of organizational complexity that automatically places it into this category, even if attendance figures and operating budget are nowhere near this size. The major organizing challenge or theme of this size category is decentralization. All of the careful work that was done to align church structures in the previous size categories suddenly seems to get in the way of a more organic leadership style needed to function in this very large category. The matrix-sized church takes its name from the shape of the organizational chart that often characterizes this church size. More will be said about that design in the paragraphs that follow.

Growth in the matrix-sized church emerges and is managed everywhere, all at the same time. Independent functional ministry areas (such as music ministry, children's ministry, or senior adult ministry) are each generating new initiatives for their constituent groups to engage. At the same time, identifiable community groups within the larger church body (the 10:00 a.m. contemporary worship community, the north campus community, the annex worship community) are each engaging their own strategic initiatives aimed at growth. On the surface, the matrix-sized congregation looks remarkably chaotic. However, when you look beneath the surface, you see that growth initiatives are coordinated through a well-executed strategic planning process and a carefully crafted operational planning and budgeting process.

The senior clergyperson of this congregation adopts a leadership style that appears even more hands off than the strategic focus described in earlier categories. I refer to effective leadership in this size category as *ideation* leadership. The senior clergy leader must focus primarily on the overall strategy of the congregation, teaching, preaching, and fundraising. She must lead the staff team and board with clear statements about vision, values, and strategic priorities. She has fully delegated the management of the staff team to one or more executive ministers, whose job it is to run the organization. Her work with the staff team is limited to the crafting of strategic messages and the support of a culture that embodies the strategic identity of the congregation.

The staff team in this size congregation requires a new organizational design. Many staff members in this structure are required to maintain a dual focus on both their functional area of responsibility and the attendant needs of multiple sites and constituencies. To this end, staff members in the matrix church often have to maintain dual supervisory relationships, giving birth to an organizational structure that is known as a matrix structure in the world of organizational design. For example, a youth minister operating at the north campus of the church is accountable to the north campus pastor, as well as to the director of youth ministries on the main campus. As a result of operating in more decentralized structures, the decision-making processes of the staff team also have to become more decentralized. The overall coordination of staff team decision making is carefully orchestrated by an executive staff team, made up of the senior pastor and the equivalent of a chief operating officer and a chief administrative officer.

In this size congregation, it is not unusual for a "kitchen cabinet" or elder leadership group to emerge. This is a five- to seven-member group of key lay leaders who advise the senior minister and executive minister. Sometimes this group is a subgroup of the governing body of the church. At other times it is a separate ad hoc advisory group with less clear constitutional authority to act. The kitchen cabinet often helps the senior clergy person to think creatively and strategically. They also work to triage presenting problems and decisions in the congregation, to make sure that the most appropriate decision-making groups are engaging each issue.

A congregation that is organized as a matrix church has a strong and effective department that tends to the welcoming and assimilation function of the church. This department works to ensure that a unified strategic identity is communicated across worship venues and campus locations. Clearly articulated and coordinated programs of welcome, orientation, discipleship, membership, and stewardship address the needs of multiple constituent bodies.

METAPHORICALLY SPEAKING

The professional church, the strategic church, and the matrix church each represent a fundamentally different operating system. I'd like to offer three different living biological systems—the caterpillar, the spider, and the starfish[3]—as examples of how differently these congregations are oriented.

Metaphorically, the professional church moves and functions like a caterpillar. A caterpillar has multiple legs that can all move on their own, but the work of those legs is highly coordinated. A caterpillar moves with a wave that starts at the back end of its body and sweeps through each segment until it reaches the head, pushing it forward. Six legs attached to the thorax of the caterpillar actually move it around. Additional pairs of prolegs support and move the length of the caterpillar's abdomen. These prolegs may look like legs but they don't have segments or joints, so that only the six real legs at the thorax move the insect.

Like the caterpillar, the professional church moves in a single coordinated motion under the guidance and direction of the staff team. The governing body is the head of the caterpillar, making choices about the direction that the organism is moving. The staff team functions as the real legs, which propel the congregation forward. Although it looks like there is a lot of independent motion in the professional church, it really is the activity of the staff team that controls and directs forward momentum.

The strategic church moves more like a spider. A spider operates with eight independent legs, and each leg has the ability to move on its own. At first glance the spider appears to move very awkwardly. With eight eyes and eight legs all working independently, it seems like a disjointed organism. However, upon further observation one can see that the overall movement of the spider is well coordinated. The head is clearly in charge, interpreting the signals received by those eight eyes and coordinating the work of those independent legs. The spider is a centralized system with well-coordinated parts working interdependently as a whole.

Like the spider, the well-run strategic church functions as a centralized system. Various departments within the church and on the staff team operate like the legs of the spider. At first glance they appear to have a great deal of independence. Upon closer inspection one can see that their movement is well coordinated. The governing body of the church, along with the executive management team, functions as the centralized decision-making force (the head) that keeps the congregation moving in alignment.

The matrix church is yet another kind of system, one I compare to the starfish. At first glance, a starfish is similar to a spider in appearance. Like the spider, the starfish appears to have a bunch of legs attached to a central body. But that is where the similarities end, because the starfish is decentralized. A starfish doesn't have a head. Its central body isn't even in charge. In fact, the major organs are replicated through every arm. If you cut an arm off, most starfish will be able to grow a new arm. In some species, if you cut the starfish in half, both sides will regenerate, and you'll have two starfish. They can achieve this magical regeneration because a starfish operates as a decentralized neural network. It doesn't have a traditional brain. There is no central command. One arm begins to move and somehow convinces each of the other arms to move with it in a process that is not yet fully understood.[4]

Like the starfish, the matrix church operates in a decentralized fashion. It would be an exaggeration to say that there is no centralized brain in the matrix church. There is a center, but it is not a command center. The governing board and executive management team craft and communicate a strong congregational identity, core values, and strategic priorities. Then, every arm of the church is free to translate that identity into a workable set of movements that do not have to be centrally coordinated. The DNA of the church is fully represented in each of the arms of the church, and each arm is free to chart its own course, provided that the DNA is honored.

If we embrace the metaphors of caterpillar, spider, and starfish to represent the fundamental orientations of the three sizes of large congregations, we can appreciate the challenge of reorganization. Consider the congregation that has functioned like a caterpillar over a sustained period of time that suddenly has to reorient itself and begin behaving like a spider. Or the starfish organization that has experienced a period of decline and now has to function more like a spider. The adaptation involves more than simply adding staff or decreasing the size of the board. Rightsizing is a fundamental shift in the way that the major leadership systems of the church operate. And the realignment has to happen across all of the same leadership systems simultaneously.

TRANSITION AND ALIGNMENT

There is always a danger in labeling size categories. The naming of threshold limits and the assignment of labels suggests a process that is much cleaner and more predictable than found in real life. Individual congregations transition in and out of these organizational paradigms in remarkably unique ways. Some congregations completely skip a size category. Most congregational leaders, when asked to identify themselves within this categorical landscape, will immediately identify with a primary zone that they believe is descriptive of their organizational and leadership challenges. But few congregational leaders believe that their systems reside within a single category. Most will say something like this: "Well, we are clearly a strategic-size congregation based upon our weekly attendance and our operating budget. And alignment is the primary organizational challenge that we are facing. But I am still providing clergy leadership that is more typically found in a professional-size congregation, and the organization of our staff team still looks like the professional-size church. Our board, unfortunately, is still behaving like the board of a multi-cell church, even though we've been this sized congregation for well over 10 years. No wonder, I'm so worn out."

Let's consider several common questions that emerge when leaders work with these size-zone designations in a diagnostic way.

What will happen if our leadership systems are organized inappropriately for our size? How big a problem is that?

I have worked with a number of thriving churches with leadership systems that are not appropriately configured for their size. Having systems that are out of sync doesn't prevent some marvelous ministry from taking place. Likewise, appropriately aligning your leadership systems won't ensure that you grow or thrive.

This is what I do know. Congregations that don't align their leadership systems spend inordinate amounts of energy trying to get things done, and the organizational problems that leaders think they have solved don't generally stay solved. Leaders are often exhausted, frustrated, or burned out by the time and energy that it takes to get simple things accomplished. Properly aligning the leadership systems of your congregation will allow you to spend your leadership energies in more fruitful ways. A congregation operating with leadership systems that are severely out of alignment will likely find that sustained future growth (however it desires to grow) is impossible.

What will happen if a congregation completely skips a size category? Will it miss some key developmental tasks that it needs to go back and pick up?

It is not unusual for a congregation that is on a rapid growth trajectory to power its way through an entire size category without doing any type of adaptation. Leaders may one day wake up and discover that the congregation has become matrix-size, while still functioning like a professional-size church. Typically when this happens, the growth is attributable to the huge charismatic presence of a single clergy leader or extraordinary growth in the community surrounding the congregation.

When this does occur, I advise congregations to get rightsized for their present setting. It isn't necessary for a congregation that skipped the strategic size zone to go back and learn those leadership systems. It's more important that they design their leadership systems to serve their present situation. A congregation that skips a size zone will have more difficulty learning the skills needed for their present size zone, but it is a doable task. For example, the strategic church learns important lessons about aligning strategy that are required for successful leadership in the matrix congregation. Church leaders still need to learn those skills, even though they don't need to live as a strategic church.

What if we are living in multiple size zones at the same time? Is that a problem?

I am not in favor of fixing things that are not broken. If your leadership systems are truly working for you, I don't think that you should jump in and realign them, just to be in sync with a chart that I've invented. However, in my experience, congregations that live simultaneously in a number of different size zones exhibit problematic symptoms. Usually, they have invented strategies for sidestepping or working around the leadership system that is hindering their progress. This almost always has unintended negative consequences.

How is the rightsizing of leadership systems in a shrinking congregation different from the rightsizing that takes place in a growing congregation?

In many respects, the rightsizing of leadership systems is the same whether the church is growing or shrinking in size. However, in a downsizing scenario the first leadership system to adapt is almost always the staff team configuration, in response to a budget crisis. Many congregations make the mistake of reducing staff size without also examining the overall role that the staff team plays in the life of the congregation, and without making corresponding adjustments in the remaining leadership systems.

A congregation going through a downsizing usually grapples with issues of negative self image. One of the best ways to help a congregation come to terms with the adequacy of their present size is to rightsize their leadership systems. Hanging onto systems that were designed for a larger congregation only reminds members of what they have lost, as they struggle to make wrong-sized structures work. Rightsizing the structure can unleash new energies by helping a struggling congregation discover their nimble selves and a newfound sense of abundance.

Should we design our leadership systems to serve the size congregation we are currently or to serve the size of congregation that we see ourselves becoming?

Your leadership systems have to serve the congregation that you presently are, and they have to serve the congregation that you are becoming. Most congregations discover that they need to begin reorganizing their leadership systems as they approach the higher end of a size zone, in anticipation of what is coming next. Congregations may find that they bounce up against an attendance zone limit over and over and can't push through until they redesign. However, if the leadership system that you design is too far out in front of your present reality, your leaders will begin experiencing other alignment problems.

Where do we begin in the process of getting ourselves rightsized?

The simplest first step is to help your current leaders develop common language for understanding the basic building blocks of church life and the nature of the five systems (both discussed in chapter 2), as well as the various size categories laid out in this chapter. Equipped with shared terminology, church leaders often find incredibly resourceful ways of getting themselves more appropriately aligned for their ministry context.

Once you've adopted some shared terminology, I'd also recommend moving on to part 2 of this text. Part 2 examines each of the five leadership systems of the church in greater detail, and illustrates the specific ways in which those systems change in response to the pressures of changing size and complexity.

QUESTIONS FOR INDIVIDUAL OR GROUP REFLECTION

1. What is the average weekend worship attendance in your congregation (counting children and their teachers in the building during worship)? Is average weekend worship attendance a good indicator of the size and complexity of your congregation, or are there other mitigating factors that result in your church behaving like a larger or smaller congregation than weekend attendance might suggest?

2. Consider whether any of the following dynamics describe ministry in your context. Do any of these features cause your congregation to behave like a bigger or smaller congregation than worship attendance might suggest?

   a. Size of your operating budget: Is your operating budget either larger or smaller than most other congregations your size?
   b. Midweek ministries: Do you operate an unusual number of midweek ministries that draw a significant number of people into your building during the week? Do these people also attend on weekends, or does the midweek community typically function independently of the weekend community?
   c. Building size and function: Is there anything unique about your campus that adds to the complexity of your organizational structure? Is your building a historical attraction? Does it operate with a family center or recreation center that is heavily utilized by the community? How does the use of your building add to the complexity of your organizational structure?

d. Number of worship venues and sites: Do you operate at multiple campuses? How many different worship venues do you host? In what ways do these features add to the complexity of your organization?

e. Affluence: How would you describe the affluence of the community that supports your congregation? In what ways does the affluence (or lack thereof) of your community place demands upon your organizational complexity?

f. Affiliated nonprofits: What nonprofits are affiliated with your congregation? In what ways is the activity and structure of your board or your staff team influenced by the presence of these nonprofits?

g. Are there other mitigating factors, besides those mentioned above, that factor into the complexity, leadership, or organizing systems of your congregation? What are they? In what ways are they affecting the congregation?

INDIVIDUAL OR GROUP EXERCISE

Refer to chart at the end of this chapter. This chart lists some of the defining characteristics of four size categories: the multi-celled church, the professional church, the strategic church, and the matrix church. The column on the left side of the chart lists various attributes, organizing themes, and leadership challenges for each size category. In the cells to the right are the attributes of various size congregations. The best way to determine the "real" size of your congregation is to determine which of the challenges described in the chart matches your lived experience.

Read through the chart and determine which size description best characterizes your congregation in each of the areas listed. Record your observation by placing a check mark in the appropriate cell in the table on the next page.

In the area of: *We behave most like this size category:*

	Multi-Cell	Professional	Strategic	Matrix
Average Attendance				
Operating Budget				
Growth Challenges				
Pastoral Challenges				
Staff Team Challenges				
Board Challenges				
Assimilation Challenges				
OVERALL				

1. Does the behavior of your congregation place you firmly within one size category, or are you straddling two or more size categories?
2. Is your congregation being pulled upward or downward along the size continuum?
3. Which leadership challenges are currently the most problematic for your congregation? Is there one set of leadership challenges that seem to be holding you back from living into the size category that feels most appropriate to you? In which system are you experiencing the most palpable level of stress?
4. What adaptations would need to take place in order for your congregation's systems to feel "rightsized"?

Size Category	The Multi-Celled Church	The Professional Church	The Strategic Church	The Matrix Church
Avg. Weekend Attendance	250–400	400–800	800–1,200	1,200–1,800
-or- Annual Operating Budget	$400,000–$1,000,000	$1,000,000–$2,000,000	$2,000,000–$4,000,000	$4,000,000 –
ORGANIZING THEME	LEADERSHIP DEVELOPMENT	PROFESSIONALIZATION	ALIGNMENT	DECENTRALIZATION
Growth Challenges	*Examine assumptions about growth* The congregation must come to terms with how it understands and defines growth, whether it desires growth, and whether the culture will accommodate growth. Leaders must claim a strategic identity and define growth accordingly.	*Build capacity for growth on the staff team* Ideas to generate growth abound but are limited by the capacity of the staff team and limitations in the facility. The church's capacity for growth is largely a function of the size of its budget.	*Assume growth and plan for it* Lack of growth will lead to stagnation and ultimately to decline. Growth is an ongoing management issue. The nature and direction of growth has to be continually negotiated and planned.	*Manage growth from multiple places* Independent functional ministry areas and locations are all working on their own growth initiatives. Growth initiatives are coordinated through the strategic planning and operational budgeting processes.
Pastoral Challenges	*Adopt a visionary leadership style* The senior clergy leader must: Discern and articulate an energizing vision for the congregation, and translate vision into specific goals to be accomplished. Clearly describe who the congregation is and is not, and what its mission is and is not. Communicate a caring presence in the congregation while reducing the level of one-on-one care provided to congregation members.	*Adopt a managerial leadership style* The senior clergy leader must: Let go of a purely relational style of leadership and engage the congregation from a managerial perspective. Shift the care focus from the congregation at large to the staff team and key lay leaders. Manage the collective performance of the staff team.	*Adopt a strategic leadership style* The senior clergy leader must: Focus on the right things, say no to the wrong things, and spend time on the important things. Let go of day-to-day management decisions, find ways to pull back and see the big picture, and learn to lead through the projection of a public persona. Crystallize the vision of the church into clear sound bites that keep the staff team and board in alignment.	*Adopt an ideation leadership style* The senior clergy leader must: Focus exclusively on strategy, teaching, preaching and fundraising Lead the staff team and board with clear statements of vision, values, and strategic priorities Create a culture that supports the generation of new ideas and innovation Delegate the day-to-day management of the church.

	The Multi-Celled Church 250–400	The Professional Church 400–800	The Strategic Church 800–1,200	The Matrix Church 1,200–1,800
Size Category **Avg. Weekend Attendance** -or- **Annual Operating Budget**	$400,000–$1,000,000	$1,000,000–$2,000,000	$2,000,000–$4,000,000	$4,000,000 +
Staff Team Challenges	*Embrace a team identity* The team must: Add specialized program staff to grow the church when the budget may not be fully ready to support staff additions. Learn to balance the work of the generalist alongside the work of the specialist.	*Professionalize the ministry* The team must: Assume tasks previously accomplished by volunteers Find new ways to engage volunteers. Move away from a generalist orientation to distinct areas of specialization. Accept supervision from someone other than the senior clergy leader.	*Align work of multiple sub-teams* Staff must: Avoid a silo mentality. Maintain a relational focus in program roles as the administrative components of roles increase. Grow the admin team to accommodate additional growth in the church. Learn to work under the direction of an executive leadership team.	*Create cross-functional structure* Staff must: Communicate and coordinate, sometimes around dual reporting relationships. Maintain a dual focus on their functional areas of responsibility, and attend to the needs of multiple sites and/or constituencies. Decentralize decision-making.
Board Challenges	*Organize work around mission* Board leaders must: Coordinate the work of a variety of committees and groups. Learn to say yes to ideas and activities that support the mission and no to ideas that distract the congregation from its mission. Develop new lay leadership.	*Create management systems* Board leaders must: Create policies and establish a staff team performance management system. Relinquish the daily management of the church to the staff team.	*Reduce size of governing board* The board must: Provide a strong support and accountability system for the head of staff. Operate with a strategic mindset, letting go of representational thinking. Create an executive team (if board size is larger than 7 people). Other leaders must: Learn to trust the decision-making lead of a smaller group.	*Decentralize decision-making* The board must: Empower each ministry venue to make decisions about growth in their own areas. Institute a systematic approach to program evaluation to keep the number of programming options workable.

Size Category	The Multi-Celled Church	The Professional Church	The Strategic Church	The Matrix Church
Avg. Weekend Attendance -or-	250–400	400–800	800–1,200	1,200–1,800
Annual Operating Budget	$400,000–$1,000,000	$1,000,000–$2,000,000	$2,000,000–$4,000,000	$4,000,000 +
Assimilation Challenges	*Expand points of entry*	*Watch the back door*	*Create a seamless system of membership*	*Coordinate participation across venues*
	The congregation must:	The congregation must:	The congregation must:	The congregation must:
	Add new worship venues, small group ministries, etc.	Address the anonymity that occurs in the large church.	Link membership, discipleship, gift discovery, and stewardship through a fully formed network of classes or small groups.	Create a membership/development department to coordinate the many venues of entry, so a unified perspective on membership is generated.
	Meet emerging standards of excellence that people expect from a larger congregation.	Find new ways to keep track of members and to get members engaged.	Add a staff member who focuses on membership and volunteer management.	Hire a development director
		Let the staff team take the lead in identifying and developing new leaders.	Empower newcomers to find their own way into participation and membership.	Customize and coordinate programs of orientation, and membership so that each venue is unique, but unified.

PART 2

Leadership Systems in Motion

CHAPTER 4

Clergy Leadership Roles

THE ROOM WAS CHARGED WITH BOTH ANXIETY AND EXCITEMENT. IT WAS late on Saturday afternoon, the closing hour of a two-day leadership retreat focused on naming the strategic priorities for the next chapter of life at Lake Street Presbyterian. This retreat was the culmination of six months of careful study that had been painstakingly designed to help the congregation think about its future and the characteristics needed in its next pastoral leader.

Leaders had been hard at work, recording all of their hopes and dreams for the future on sheets of newsprint taped to the walls of the room. An informal voting process had just begun to prioritize the many dreams articulated over the course of the weekend. A nervous giddiness settled over the room as leaders quieted down to hear the top vote getters, those ideas that had risen like cream to the top of the list. The predictable strategic priorities emerged first:

- We need to deepen and enhance youth ministry in our congregation. (The group responded with a resounding affirmation that this was indeed a critical priority for moving forward.)
- We need to awaken the congregation's appreciation for, and skill base in, evangelism, learning to share the good news of the Gospel and Lake Street Pres. (This too was followed by another round of affirmation.)
- We must develop the congregation's understanding of, and commitment to, stewardship. ("Of course, we can't go

forward without fuller financial support and deeper engagement of our entire membership!")

And then . . .

- We need to find a new senior minister that everyone will love and support! (You could have cut the silence in the room with a knife.)

The consultant facilitating the event stepped forward and drew a large red circle around this last item on the wall. She stepped back and made the following observation, "This is an impossible statement, and I can't, in good conscience, let you select this particular statement as one of your new strategic priorities. We need to find a healthier way to talk about the aspirations behind this statement."

The room exploded with a fury of observations about what the statement really meant and what was realistic to expect. The conversation was emotionally charged and carried the full pent-up frustration of a leadership body that had endured months of pain and conflict around pastoral leadership. Ultimately, what the group decided they wanted to say was this:

- We need an effective and healthy transition to a new senior pastorate that will be characterized by these attributes:
  o Clear and realistic expectations about the essential functions of the senior pastor role and the core competencies needed for someone to lead this congregation through its next chapter;
  o Clarity about the congregation's hopes and dreams for the future;
  o Transparency between leaders and members about the selection process;
  o Transparency between the pastor nominating committee and potential candidates about our core identity, hopes and dreams, and weaknesses;
  o An effective vetting of the new candidate that allows leaders to evaluate fit with congregational culture; and

o A realistic recognition that no candidate will appeal to everyone, combined with a healthy respect for the opinions of those who don't personally affirm the new candidate.

Let's look at the background that produced this moment. Lake Street Presbyterian is a church that prides itself on a history of long pastorates. Only five senior pastors have served the congregation in its 100-year history. This is a place where clergy finish out their careers. Leaders arrive early in their careers and stay until retirement, investing long years of vibrant service. At least that was the pattern until the most recent pastorate, which was a failed 18-month experience. The most recent senior pastor left under pressure in the midst of chaos, confusion, and bad behavior on the part of many typically well-behaved people.

Since the senior pastor's departure, many have speculated about what went wrong. Wildly different stories have emerged explaining a variety of errors on the part of both pastor and congregation. Some loved him and others believed he was a disastrous choice for the role. Everyone agrees that the mismatch of pastor and congregation produced devastating consequences for all involved. Church membership, attendance, and budgets have all taken a huge hit these past three years. The pastor and his family were wounded. Leadership relationships were strained, in some cases beyond repair. Church leaders tell themselves that the congregation cannot endure another bad fit between congregation and pastor. They must "get it right" this time, or the congregation will experience irreversible consequences.

During the retreat, leaders took a painfully honest look at their history leading up to the most recent senior pastorate. Before the retreat, leaders often said the congregation had been thriving in every way before the arrival of the previous senior pastor. In fact, an honest retelling of history prompted the realization that the decline of the congregation had begun well over 15 years earlier. The congregation's emotional attachment to the senior pastor immediately prior to this one had prevented people from paying attention to the long downward slide that had begun back in that era.

In fact, today Lake Street Presbyterian is a significantly smaller congregation than it was 20 years ago. It is still a large church that would fit the professional size category discussed in this book. It used to reside firmly in the strategic size category. However, expectations about the leadership role of the senior pastor have changed little over that long, slow, downward size transition. People still believe that the next senior pastor needs to present an electric persona in the pulpit and should be regarded as a national figurehead in the denomination. They want both warmth and intellectual stimulation. They believe that the right kind of preacher will "pack them in" once again, and life will be good at Lake Street Pres.

In reflecting upon the story of Lake Street Presbyterian (and most of the other large congregations I work with), I can't help but draw a comparison between the expectations of congregants in large congregations and the familiar family story, *Mary Poppins*. Okay, it's a stretch, but bear with me on this one. In the Disney version of the story, we meet Jane and Michael Banks, a rather energetic and sometimes naughty pair of kids with a penchant for chewing up and spitting out nannies. As the movie opens, yet another nanny has departed from the Banks household, and the parents are up in arms about what to do. In the midst of the chaos, Jane and Michael approach their father and angelically present (in song, of course) a list of the attributes that they would like to see in their next nanny. The list is amusingly long and describes a caregiver who couldn't possibly exist in real life. Mr. Banks rips up the letter in exasperation and sends the children off to bed.

The very next day, Mary Poppins magically appears, born on the wings of a mysterious wind. One of her first acts as nanny is to measure the children to determine their character strengths and flaws. She pulls out a magical tape measure to assist with the task. After carefully assessing the children, Mary Poppins turns the magical tape measure on herself and reads, "Mary Poppins: Practically perfect in every way." And so, the story unfolds of how this practically perfect and magically mysterious nanny restores order, hope, and love to an impossible household.

Like the Banks household, we too come with our impossible lists of character attributes that we lay at the feet of senior clergy leaders. We expect them to be every bit as magical as Mary Poppins, restoring order, hope, and love to otherwise unruly households.

Some congregations are lucky and actually do manage to find just the right combination of attributes in a clergy leader, one who also fits well with the culture of the congregation, and they live in relationship with one another in a way that feels rather magical. Others, when they find out that the senior clergy leader is not as wonderful as hoped for, turn on that leader, spit him or her out, and set out again in search of the perfectly magical person who can make the world right again.

Setting unrealistic expectations is not unique to the large congregation. Small and mid-sized congregations hope for their share of magic as well. What is different in the large congregation is the intensity of expectations around the "practically perfect" part. The larger a congregation becomes, the greater the unarticulated expectations become, and the less likely that people will actually know the senior leader in any real way. There is a common misperception in the world of congregations that larger churches are served by those pastors who have proven themselves "most perfect" in other settings, thus warranting appointment to the large congregation, and that the larger a congregation becomes, the more perfect the senior clergy leader required to lead it.

In fact, effective senior clergy in large congregations are far from perfect, and most of them would be the first to say so. Being an effective clergy leader (whether the senior, an associate, or an executive clergy leader) depends upon the person clearly understanding the competencies that the role requires, developing those competencies, spending time on the right things, and fitting well within the culture of the congregation.

How does the size of a congregation determine the role of the senior clergy person and the competencies of the person needed to fill the role? What is fundamentally different about the attributes required of senior clergy in a church with 300 in worship, compared to the senior leader of a congregation with 1,000 in worship? What is different about how those two leaders spend their time? These are the initial questions that we will seek to answer in this chapter. Then we will go on to explore the roles of associate clergy and how those roles are played out differently in different sized congregations. Finally, we'll look at the role of the executive pastor, a role that is unique to the large congregation. We'll examine what the role is designed to do and examine the markers that suggest when a congregation is ready for an executive pastor.

The Senior Clergy Role

A common assumption about the large church leader is that she can learn the skills needed to do the job by serving well in a variety of small and medium-sized congregations or as a middle judicatory leader. Most of our denominational systems act as if this were true. The vocational trajectory of pastors is often targeted at landing progressively larger congregations. Encouragement to follow this trajectory comes from the increase in salaries that clergy receive by taking on ever-bigger churches.

Unfortunately, success as a pastor of a small or mid-sized congregation is no guarantee of success in leading a large congregation. Leadership in the large congregation calls upon skill sets different from those required to lead in the small to medium-sized congregation. Most leaders of large congregations have, in fact, first proven themselves in smaller settings. However, many outstanding pastors of small to mid-sized congregations are not well suited for leadership in the large congregation, and would not even enjoy the role. Let's look at why this is true.

Core Competencies of Senior Clergy

What are the critical competencies needed to effectively lead a large congregation? Core competencies are the skills, personal attributes, and behavioral patterns that leaders need to demonstrate daily. Competencies do not describe the tasks required to carry out the role but the skills, attributes, and behaviors used in the execution of the role.

The following list represents my personal assessment of the top ten competencies that effective senior clergy must possess to lead the large congregation. With this list I am not trying to make distinctions between the leadership of the professional, strategic, and matrix-sized congregations. I am simply lifting up those leadership competencies that stand out among effective large-church leaders, particularly when compared to leadership in the small-to-mid-sized congregation.

1. **Decision-Making Skills:** Makes effective, timely decisions, balancing analysis and intuition; recognizes the short and long-term implications of choices made; defines problems and issues clearly, offers solutions and suggestions that are efficient and pragmatic; evaluates when to make a decision under conditions of risk and uncertainty and when to wait for better information.

2. **Ego Strength:** Demonstrates strong and appropriate personal boundaries in relationships; appreciates the distinctiveness and value of self, without being arrogant; is spiritually and emotionally mature; maintains a nonanxious presence in the midst of turmoil; does not overly depend upon outside affirmation; maintains a strong personal support system.

3. **Organizational Agility:** Is astute about how congregations work; knows how to get things done through board, team, and committee structures as well as through informal relationship networks; understands the importance of supporting good policy, practice, and procedure; appreciates the power in the culture of a congregation; is politically astute.

4. **Personal Resilience:** Learns from adversity and failure; discerns when to change personal, interpersonal, and managerial behaviors; deals well with ambiguity; copes effectively with change; comfortably handles risk and uncertainty; seeks feedback; expresses personal regret when appropriate; demonstrates a strong spiritual centeredness.

5. **Preaching and Worship Leadership Skills:** Is a consistently effective preacher and worship leader; inspires from the pulpit; communicates a clear and consistent message through sermons that are carefully prepared and artfully delivered; projects the identity and character of the congregation through his or her presence as a worship leader.

6. **Process Management Skills:** Designs practices, processes, and procedures that allow managing from a distance; understands how to create efficient work flow; knows what to

measure and how to measure it; identifies opportunities for synergy and integration; simplifies complex processes.

7. **Public Presence:** Demonstrates a comfortable ease in speaking in a variety of settings (both small and large groups, inside and outside the congregation); knows how to be strongly present in the room without commanding the room; effectively addresses both straightforward data and controversial topics; projects a clear sense of congregational identity through personal demeanor.

8. **Strategic Leadership Skills:** Is future oriented and can articulate a clear picture of the congregation's preferred future; effectively involves others in the discernment of the vision; identifies and prioritizes strategic objectives that are consistent with the vision of the congregation; keeps staff and lay leaders focused on critical priorities; prevents vision drift.

9. **Supervision Skills:** Is good at establishing clear expectations and setting clear direction; sets stretching objectives; distributes the workload appropriately; delegates effectively; provides regular and ongoing feedback about performance; proactively deals with substandard performance; engages disciplinary processes in a timely manner.

10. **Team Orientation:** Identifies and recruits good talent for the team; sets clear strategic direction for the team; negotiates team difficulties, including the conflict that emerges around diversity and inclusion issues; creates strong morale and spirit; shares wins and successes; creates a feeling of belonging and pride in the team.

The casual observer reading this list of competencies may remark, "With the exception of preaching, this list looks like it could be written for leadership in just about any large organization." And that assessment is pretty accurate. The large congregation is a complex nonprofit and requires the leadership savvy and skill set that would be required to effectively lead any large organization.

The list is remarkable not only for what it contains, but for what it omits. Notice that the list does not include many of the tasks typically associated with clergy leadership: pastoral care, visitation, social justice witness, and spiritual formation. In the small church the clergy leader tends to the ministry of the congregation by performing acts of pastoral care, visitation, social justice witness, and discipleship. In the large church, the senior clergy indirectly tends to these ministries by managing systems that carry out each ministry. Performing the act yourself requires remarkably different competencies from supervising others who perform the act.

Essential Functions of Senior Clergy Leadership

The essential functions address the "what?" question of leadership. They are the duties and tasks required in the role. *What* do the senior clergy of congregations actually focus on each day? How should they be investing their time? One of the greatest challenges of large church leadership is figuring out where to focus attention and what to disengage from. Let's listen to the voices of three large church clergy leaders as they describe the dilemma of time management in the senior clergy role.

Pastor 1
When I first came here, the incessant onslaught of demands on my attention was overwhelming. Every question and detail was directed my way. I didn't have a set of criteria for what I would pay attention to. I had to learn to build a list of things to which my automatic response was, "No, I won't do that." As a senior pastor in a large church you will make four or five key decisions over the course of your tenure that will impact the life of the church; these are decisions that no one else can make. You'll miss them if you are overfocusing on detail.

Pastor 2
Knowing when to say no is critical. In a big congregation there seems to be no end of opportunities for new and different things to do. Lots of them are things that are possible. The question is, are they the right things to do? It's easy to get scattered and lose the congregation's sense of focus by saying yes to everything. When that happens, there is no unifying theme to what is happening. Busyness happens without real progress. Being able to say no, based on genuine priorities, is critical.

Pastor 3
When I hit my overwhelm level, it's a barometer about when the church is ready to grow into a new stage. I have come to recognize when I am anxious and have come to understand that I am carrying the anxiety of the church—or whatever its emotions are. I'm the triage nurse. I am constantly reordering my priorities. It's very hard to practice discernment with any kind of intention. I know that whatever I put my focus on will probably grow. If I pay attention to a problem, it will grow. If I pay attention to a conflicted situation, it almost always grows. If I get busy doing something else, the conflict often goes away.

One of the questions I am most frequently asked by my coaching clients is, "How should I be spending my time?" My answer to them is always some version of this statement: "You need to spend your time on those things that are uniquely yours to do by virtue of your role. You need to let go of those things that would be better accomplished by others."

The question of which duties and tasks are the senior clergy leader's to own can't be answered universally for all large congregations. The size zone within which a congregation resides makes a big difference in how the senior clergy leader focuses her time. Let's look at our three sizes of large to better understand the time management of the senior clergy leader.

The Senior Clergy Leader in the Professional Church

The small to mid-size church pastor manages the life of the congregation by managing relationships and tasks. In the smaller church things often get done because the pastor does them. The pastor focuses on individual relationships as the primary means to coordinate and facilitate the ministry of the congregation.

In the professional-size congregation, the effective senior clergy leader has learned to substitute this primarily relational style with a more managerial style. This pastor has shifted his leadership focus away from individuals in the congregation and more towards the board, the staff team, and key lay leaders. Having said that, the senior clergy leader is still viewed by most people in the congregation as "their" pastor, and the demands on her time for weddings, funerals, and pastoral care visits is still great.

She is managing the performance of the congregation by facilitating staff team and board work. She is creating and sustaining the performance management cycle of the congregation through goal setting, budgeting, performance review, and a coaching leadership style.

Senior clergy leaders in this size congregation are often amazed at how much of their time is spent in administration and staff supervision, some estimating that as much of 85 percent of their time is spent on management. Preaching is an important task but never seems to get the time it deserves with all of the administrative tasks that need to be tended in an average week.

The Senior Clergy Leader in the Strategic Church
The hallmark of senior clergy leadership in this size congregation is the need for a more strategic mindset. This size congregation operates with multiple supervisory levels (see chapter 5), so the senior clergy leader has fewer direct reports than in the professional church. This means that she is spending less time daily in direct supervision than the senior clergy leader in the professional-size church.

This size congregation often operates as a conglomeration of small congregations, each with its own identified clergy leader. The Saturday evening worshiping community may think of the clergy leader who regularly leads that service as "their" pastor. The Sunday morning 8:30 a.m. service also has its identified clergy leader. Consequently, not everyone in the congregation considers the senior clergy leader to be their personal pastor, which means that time demands around weddings, funerals, and pastoral care aren't as oppressive as they are for the professional-church senior clergy leader.

At some point in this size category, the congregation likely forms executive teams, one within the staff team and one within the board structure. (Some congregations form a single executive team that leads both the board and the staff team.) The senior clergy leader focuses much of his time on these leadership groups.

The strategic church pastor must increasingly learn to say no to good ideas that aren't right for the moment, so the staff team and governing board don't lose their focus. The strategic church pastor is always struggling to keep his focus on the dance floor, but from the perspective of the balcony. He is looking to personify the mission and vision of the congregation in everything he says and does. He is the primary connecting link between various sub-teams within the larger staff team, continually looking for ways to connect groups and cross-fertilize ideas. He is still involved in important decision making but often only indirectly, through the work he does with his direct reports.

The preaching task becomes increasingly important the larger the congregation becomes. The amount of time that the senior clergy leader spends in study and sermon preparation grows with each increase in size category.

Increasingly, the pastor in this size congregation works as venture capitalist/fundraiser for the congregation. In this congregation great new ideas are always in some stage of development that requires additional funding. The senior clergy leader is constantly managing the relationship between the congregation and its donors.

The Senior Clergy Leader in the Matrix Church

The senior clergy leader of the matrix-size congregation adopts a leadership focus and style that appears even more hands off than the previous category. I refer to effective leadership in this size category as ideation leadership. The senior clergy leader must focus primarily on the overall vision and strategy of the congregation, teaching, preaching, and fundraising. She must lead the staff team and board with clear statements of vision, values, and strategic priorities. The pastor in this size congregation may identify more strongly with the labels of teacher, writer, and community leader than with the identity of shepherd or pastor.

This leader has fully delegated the management of the staff team to one or more executive ministers, whose job it is to run the organization. This senior clergy leader rarely attends staff meetings beyond the executive team meeting, other than as a vision-casting presence at "all staff" gatherings. Her work with the staff team is limited to crafting strategic messages and supporting the strategic identity of the congregation (see chapter 8). She is rarely involved in staff team decision making but is closely informed about what is happening through the executive pastor(s). She retains veto rights in most decision-making processes but rarely uses them.

This senior clergy leader tends to spend a great deal of time representing the congregation in the community, at important denominational gatherings, and in the media. This pastor's writing often shows up in important publications. The preaching task is so important in this size congregation that she requires regular focused study time away from the buzz of the office to sustain it.

Planning and executing capital campaigns are hugely time consuming for this senior clergy leader. The burden of the "personal ask" rests squarely on the shoulders of this leader, and the commensurate need to maintain good relationships with key givers is an important part of the role.

Administration as Ministry

Simply reading through the earlier list of core competencies demonstrates how prevalent administration is in the role of the large church pastor. At some point, senior clergy leaders must come to terms with the idea that administration is a form of ministry. Those who cannot understand administration as ministry quickly burn out in the role, always frustrated as they try to get administration "out of the way," so they can get back to the "real" tasks of ministry.

I often work with senior clergy on the tasks of staffing and supervision in the large church. I'm struck by how often those leaders fall into the trap of thinking that supervision is something you have to do only when things aren't going well. They believe that if people would just do what they were supposed to do, then senior clergy could spend less time providing administrative oversight and more time doing "real" ministry. The seasoned large church clergy leader generally comes to see the work of supervision as sacred work that takes time to do well. Such leaders come to understand that they will always spend a significant portion of their time (at least 30 percent) on the task of staff supervision. They have the choice of spending that time in a reactive way (putting out the fires that emerge around poor supervision) or spending that time proactively guiding the strategic direction of the staff team. Crafting a culture that supports collaborative and accountable performance management is holy work that the senior clergy leader must do. In fact, there are aspects of that job that only the senior clergy leader can do.

In the book *All for God's Glory: Redeeming Church Scutwork*, Louis Weeks, president emeritus of Union Theological Seminary in Richmond, writes insightfully about the role of administration in pastoral work:

> Church administration is exceedingly complex. It consists of obvious tasks: making and keeping budgets; planning and assessing programs and activities; organizing worship and work efforts; enlisting officers, teachers, and staff, as well as dismissing those who cannot effectively carry out their responsibilities. But it also consists of subtle and systemic perspectives, for good planning makes for excellent worship and nurture; mission and witness are inextricable from effective organization; deep, trusting partnership among pastor, staff, and lay leadership are built on keeping promises and meeting responsibilities.[1]

Most of the senior clergy I work with, even the most effective ones, struggle on some level with the balance between administration and more traditional forms of ministry. In the professional size category, senior clergy leaders often grapple with how much of the administrative task to leave with boards, committees, and lay leaders in the congregation, so the clergy can engage more fully in ministry. In the strategic church pastors struggle with when and if they should hire a chief operating officer or administrative pastor to free themselves up for more strategic leadership tasks.

Many pastors struggle to determine whether a chief executive officer mantle is suited for leading the church. Many still want to think of themselves as pastors first but recognize that their role usually doesn't lend itself to pastoral kinds of activities. All senior clergy leaders grapple with how to appropriately engage in pastoral care for their size congregation and how much time to spend on preaching and teaching. Even pastors within a year of retirement will often articulate their as yet unresolved struggle about when to get personally engaged in pastoral care. The choices made always seem to come with a dose of guilt and grief as pastors struggle with not personally knowing the individual challenges and triumphs of their congregants. Most struggle with ways to articulate their sense of responsibility for the business of the church and their pastor's heart for the people of the church.

Pastor as Fundraiser

The larger the congregation becomes, the more time that the senior clergy leader will spend in fundraising. There are always new programs in need of funding. A new capital campaign is always just around the corner, and the senior clergy leader is instrumental in the success of the "big ask," particularly as it relates to the more moneyed members. The pastor of the strategic and matrix size congregation must be able to view fundraising as a form of ministry, or he will be frustrated by the demands of the role. The pastor must personally demonstrate the connection between stewardship and ministry and must invite people to connect giving with their faith.

David Ruhe, long time senior minister of Plymouth Congregational Church, describes the inherent tension in this way:

> I've done capital campaigns before (I've also had a colonoscopy more than once), but I'm still looking for a silver bullet, a magic bag of tricks, a way to make it easier, a way that doesn't feel quite so exposed when I'm sitting down with folks of means and sharing my passion for what we're doing. The closer it gets the more I want all the insight I can get into what works. And so even now I find it a challenge to address the issue of "Stewardship and Fundraising as Ministry."
>
> . . . I'd find it convenient to believe that all the stewardship and fundraising we can accomplish is ministry. But I suspect the truth is that sometimes it is and sometimes it isn't, and sorting through the differences can be challenging and painful.

Talk about stewardship carries with it a built-in conflict of interest. It's one thing to say to people, "For the good of your soul you need to find a new relationship with your stuff." It's a very different thing to say, "For the good of your soul, you need to give some of your stuff to me." I understand that we're trying very hard not to be saying the latter. But just right now the temptations are pretty powerful, and every seduction begins with a seduction of the self.[2]

In the large church the staff team becomes systematic over time about providing pastoral care coverage for various constituencies within the congregation. Each clergy leader adopts a particular constituency group for whom he is the primary pastoral care provider. Sometimes this segmentation is developed very intentionally, and at other times it occurs more organically. One of the inevitable shifts that occur as a congregation grows larger is that the senior clergy leader tends to become the pastoral care provider to the more moneyed members in the congregation. Initially, this may feel awkward or even distasteful to a senior clergy leader who does not want to think that he or she spends more time with people simply because they have money.

Effective clergy leaders have told me that the closer relationship with moneyed members seems to evolve naturally over time. As the senior clergy leader spends more time on fundraising, he tends to become the staff member who has the most frequent contact with moneyed members. This isn't necessarily a forced relationship. In fact, most senior clergy leaders tell me that these relationships tend to develop very naturally by virtue of time spent together in leadership and in reflecting on the spiritual and fiscal needs of the congregation. Because the more moneyed members have a closer working relationship with the senior clergy leader, the senior clergy leader is often the pastor of choice in moments of crisis and need. Because wealthy individuals are so often known because of their money, they crave relationships that are more authentic and genuinely spiritual. The senior clergy leader of the large congregation has a unique opportunity to tend to the spiritual and pastoral needs of these constituents in a way that is genuine and honors the relationship, beyond the boundaries of money.

Communicating Presence without Being Present

In each successively larger size category, the pastor becomes more removed from members and eventually even removed from the staff team. The larger the church becomes, the more organizational levels between the pastor and her congregants/staff/board. At the same time, the larger the congregation becomes, the more people look to the senior clergy leader to determine whether they like the church. Congregants determine whether they feel attracted to the congregation on the basis of the senior clergy's personal demeanor as presented from the public pulpit. This paradoxical combination of circumstances (further removed, but more identified with) creates a strange kind of celebrity for senior clergy leaders. It means that they have to communicate a caring and available presence, even when they are not easily accessible. Without getting absorbed into an abundance of individual relationships and without spending too much time in meetings, the senior clergy leader must communicate a sense of being fully in the know, fully attached, fully compassionate, and available. How do clergy leaders do that?

I have posed this question to countless senior clergy leaders in large congregations. Their answers are remarkably different. Each leader seems to find her own approach to communicating a sense of her availability and presence while protecting her time and privacy. Here are some of the common thematic approaches reported:

- Having a good executive assistant (EA) helps tremendously. A good EA communicates a caring and compassionate presence while fiercely protecting the time of the senior clergy leader. The EA's effectiveness in this role is often attributed to the senior clergy leader, and people give the senior clergy credit for the EA's tender care. A good EA will also keep a clergy leader well informed about what is happening among members and will direct the leader when a personal contact is needed.
- Working the worship space on Sunday mornings is critical. A well-placed handshake, a thoughtful question, a warm smile, and a remembered name will promote a strong sense of accessibility.

- Going broader, not deeper, in relationships is essential. Here is a particular technique that one pastor described to me: "Any member of the congregation can make an appointment to see me . . . once. The entire time that I am with him or her, I try to be fully present. I try to communicate that I have nothing more important to do than to be with that person in that moment. No other task of the church is as important as that meeting. But the entire time that I am with that person, I am also listening intently to determine who among my staff members is best suited for follow up and for providing further care. I don't end the session without helping this person see where they can go in the church for more support and connection. Before the end of that first session, I point him or her to someone else for further help."

A person with a pastoral heart often prefers to nurture fewer/ deeper relationships, but in fact the large church pastor needs to focus on more contacts with less depth of care. This kind of pastoral interaction is not attractive to all clergy. Not all clergy are wired to lead large congregations.

Dealing with Celebrity

The number of people who hear, and consequently feel that they personally know, the senior clergy leader is significant. She is often recognized and called out in public settings, perhaps being addressed very familiarly by people she's never personally met. In smaller church settings the pastor's spouse and family are an integral part of the ministry. In large church settings the pastor's family is often unknown and even ignored.

While people cherish falling in love with the pastor of a large church, they are also notorious for turning on the large church pastor quickly, and for no apparent reason, because there is no real relationship to draw upon. Large church pastors learn quickly not to trust the celebrity and fame. As one participant stated, "The larger a church gets, the more misunderstood you can be. People attribute motives to you when they don't even know you. It's very easy to personalize it, but you can't."

Another pastor explained the celebrity status in this way: "What I've learned: they'll turn on you in an instant. They will project any shortcoming of the church onto the leader. Don't trust the celebrity status. You just tolerate it. You pay your dues with it, you give the people that approach you the moment of attention that they need, and then you move on. If you rely on it to prop up your ego, that's a toothpick arrangement that won't stand up over time."

And finally, pastors talk about the loneliness that comes with the celebrity phenomenon. "The bigger a church gets, the lonelier it becomes as a leader. You don't know everybody anymore, but they think they know you. People assume that you are too busy to meet with them, and they no longer reach out to you. They reach out to members of your staff team instead."

The Invisible Family

Recently, after speaking to a group of pastors about clergy roles in the large church, I was approached by a senior minister who said, "I'm surprised that you didn't talk about the unique family dynamics that occur for clergy leaders of very large congregations, you know . . . the invisibility factor." I stood there looking rather dumbstruck for a few moments because, frankly, I didn't know what he was referring to.

The senior pastor went on to talk about how differently the stress of family life manifests itself in the large church. As he talked I began to recognize the phenomenon he was describing. I had encountered the issue before in other congregations with other clergy leaders; I just hadn't heard it referred to as invisibility. I immediately recognized the phenomenon as something real and profound for clergy families in large congregations.

In the small to mid-sized church, the pastor and his or her family learn to live in a fishbowl. Everything that the pastor's spouse and children do is subject to the intense scrutiny of the congregation, which places incredible pressure upon the family system. Most clergy families learn how to be clergy families in this fishbowl kind of environment. It becomes a way of life. They are accustomed to being known and watched by everyone in the congregation. The pastor's spouse learns to view himself or herself as a partner in the ministry and is often treated as the "first spouse" of the church family. Many clergy spouses in the small to mid-sized church are viewed as equal ministry partners alongside their ordained spouse. They function as unpaid clergy leaders. For better or worse, they tend to be vocationally identified with their spouse's role. Some clergy spouses thrive in the fishbowl, and others wilt under the scrutiny and the expectations.

Clergy family life in the large church is a different kind of experience. In the very large church the pastor's family assumes a cloak of invisibility. The senior clergy leader who occupies the pulpit in the large church is a persona; everyone knows or feels like he or she knows the preacher. It's difficult for the primary preacher in the large church to go out in public places without being recognized. He or she is always on display, being watched from a close distance by those who occupy the pews on Sunday morning.

At the same time, the preacher's family is having a very different kind of experience. Few people recognize or know the spouse of the senior clergy leader, unless he or she appears at the side of the clergy leader. For many clergy families, being able to step out of the fishbowl is a welcome relief. Life feels a little more normal without the close scrutiny that comes from being known as the pastor's significant others. In other families, the loss of identity can be devastating. If a clergy spouse has vocationally identified with the role of clergy spouse, the loss of identity can result in the loss of validation. Suddenly, the clergy spouse is not the significant other when attending church functions. The clergy leader may be sharing his experience of church life more intensely and directly with other clergy leaders on the staff team and not with the spouse at home. The spouse begins to feel unimportant to the ministry and left out. It seems like the ministry has become centered around "the pastor" and not at all about the family. I've even heard some leaders talk about the confusion (and hurt) that takes place within a marriage when newcomers to a congregation assume that the male senior clergy leader is married to the female associate clergy leader, simply because they occupy a shared vocational space.

The fishbowl dilemma and the invisibility dilemma represent polar opposites on the same continuum of clergy family life. Each end of the continuum hosts its own set of problems.

About Ego

When I began my work with the Alban Institute, my first project involved conducting phone interviews with senior clergy leaders of 30 large congregations (all Alban clients) in an effort to better understand their leadership challenges. At the end of the second full day of interviews, I remember calling my supervisor to express some reservation about this large church practice that Alban hoped I would craft. The problem was that I didn't like many of the people I was interviewing, or at least I didn't like something that I was hearing expressed in the interviews. Many of them demonstrated healthy egos that I experienced as arrogance in those early conversations.

I began to wonder what the large church ego persona was all about. Do most large church pastors in fact possess large egos? Have they developed large egos before they step into large congregations, or does the ego show up after the fact? Does ego go hand in hand with arrogance? Does a large ego somehow serve the senior clergy of large congregations well? In other words, do they need large egos to effectively engage or survive the role?

Over time, I have discovered that the distribution of arrogance among large church pastors is not much different from the distribution of arrogance among small and mid-sized pastors. Some are arrogant, many are not. Many of the largest congregations I have consulted with these past five years are led by remarkably humble senior leaders. I have also come to appreciate the presence of, and the need for, a good dose of ego strength (not arrogance) to effectively serve in the large congregation. Really effective pastors seem to figure out how to manifest ego strength and humility as part of the same package. Less effective pastors get sidetracked into demonstrating arrogance along with their ego.

Let's revisit the definition presented earlier for the competency of ego strength:

> Demonstrates strong and appropriate personal boundaries
> in relationships; appreciates the distinctiveness and value
> of self, without being arrogant; is spiritually and emotion-
> ally mature; maintains a nonanxious presence in the midst
> of turmoil; does not overly depend upon outside affirma-
> tion; maintains a strong personal support system.

One could make an argument that all church pastors need ego strength. However, some dimensions of large church leadership require ego strength above and beyond levels required in smaller sized congregations. The pastoral role in the large church is decid-edly different. The pastor's relationship with the congregation is not managed via one-on-one teaching and pastoral care relation-ships but is projected as a persona from the pulpit and large group teaching platforms. From the very essence of her or his being, the large church pastor must communicate an identity for the church. Because large church leadership is more publicly than personally based, it is much easier for people to distort the relationship and turn on the pastor for reasons that have nothing to do with the pastor. Conversely, the pastor may also be placed on an unrealistic pedestal. The large church pastor must have rather significant ego strength to withstand the ups and downs of this public leadership role, to avoid being held hostage by public opinion, and to rise above the isolation of being visible to many while known to very few.

Of course, I must also go on to acknowledge that some large church pastors develop a tremendous sense of arrogance along with the required ego strength. They operate with an aggravated sense of self-importance and self-worth. And I often find myself wondering why the two seem inextricably bound. Isn't it possible to develop healthy ego strength without becoming arrogant?

Here's what I've noticed about those who wander into arro-gance. They start believing that the public persona is real. They begin believing that they are the fully embodied essence of the leadership presence that others project onto them. Granted, some of the adulation is deserved. Most large church pastors possess remarkable preaching and teaching skills that garner a lot of at-tention. But I've yet to meet a real pastor who fully embodies all of the leadership qualities attached to the pulpit presence. Those who remain humble in the role are constantly working to self-correct the public image, so it more genuinely represents the real person. They manage to do this without diminishing the authority of the role or lessening the ego strength required to wear the mantle of large church leadership. Those who cross over the line into arrogance spend more of their time tending to the preservation of the public persona. They begin thinking that the public persona and the real person are one and the same.

A senior clergy leader whom I really admire once told me, "When you step into large church leadership, everyone will tell you that the success of the church and the ministry is all about you. It's not about you. Your job is to continually remind yourself and others of that important point."

ASSOCIATE CLERGY ROLES

Audrey and Libby are associate pastors serving mainline Protestant churches in the same city.[3] Both enjoy their roles, and both are considered effective in ministry. The challenges of life in associate ministry produce an immediate bond between Audrey and Libby when they meet at denominational gatherings. The two associates often discuss the challenges of leading without being the primary vision-caster and without having regular access to the pulpit. Each struggles to claim authority for her ministry, while also demonstrating commitment to the leadership of the senior pastor. Both have had the experience of being pitted against the senior pastor in a triangulated relationship, thanks to the manipulation of an unhealthy congregation member.

Although these two associates share similar role identities, they face remarkably different challenges in their roles. Audrey is the associate pastor in a church with a weekend worshiping community of 375. Libby is an associate pastor in a congregation with a weekend worshiping community of 850. Both churches are considered large. However, congregational size differences significantly shape their associate ministry roles.

The Generalist

Let's begin with Audrey's role as the single associate pastor on staff in her congregation. Audrey and her senior pastor are the only full-time clergy on the staff team. Several other part-time ministry professionals round out the staff team by providing program guidance in the areas of music ministry, children's ministry, and youth ministry, and there are several administrative support persons.

Audrey is a generalist. She bears specific ministry responsibilities for adult discipleship and religious education in the church, but she is also expected to help lead worship each week, engage in regular pastoral care responsibilities, teach regularly, preach occasionally, and attend all board meetings. Along with the senior pastor, Audrey carries responsibility for the full membership base of the congregation. The activities that Audrey engages in parallel the activities of the senior pastor, and she often takes direction from the senior pastor about how to do her job. In any given week her priorities shift considerably, given the availability and changing expectations of the senior pastor.

Serving as the second generalist on staff sometimes creates role confusion for Audrey. She receives conflicting signals about how she should be spending her time and focusing her efforts. The senior pastor seems to have one set of expectations, congregational leaders have another, and she has her own set of hopes and dreams for the position. Sometimes her role feels like the dumping ground for everything that doesn't fit someplace else in the church. And sometimes she feels like the senior pastor snatches away parts of her role, just when she is starting to make some inroads into meaningful ministry. People expect a great deal from her ministry, yet someone is always challenging the legitimacy of her decisions.

Audrey thinks of her position as developmental. She is relatively new in ministry and hopes someday to lead a large congregation of her own. She enjoys the associate role, most of the time, and feels that she is learning a great deal by observing both the successes and mistakes of her senior minister. She expects close direction from the senior leader. Audrey would like to serve as an associate for another two years, but then she hopes to step into a solo or senior pastorate of her own.

The Specialist

Libby experiences some of the same frustrations in associate ministry that Audrey reports. However, the size of Libby's congregation (850 in average weekend attendance) creates a different set of role challenges and expectations. Libby is one of twenty-five members of her staff team and one of four ordained clergy on the team. Each associate minister in the church operates with a specialized portfolio of responsibility. Libby is the associate minister of discipleship and spiritual formation. She regularly shares in pastoral care visits with other ordained staff, occasionally leads worship, and rarely preaches. Her ministry focuses only on the adult members in her congregation. Other members of the staff team carry responsibility for the spiritual formation of children and youth.

Developmental is not a word that Libby uses to describe her position. She sees the role as a vocational destination. Libby spent many years honing her skills and abilities in the area of spiritual formation and has done postgraduate work in spiritual direction. She has no desire to serve in the capacity of head of staff, now or in the foreseeable future. She doesn't want the burden of weekly preaching and staff team administration to take her away from her first love in ministry.

Libby takes overall direction from her senior pastor regarding the strategic priorities of the congregation and her position. Beyond that she operates in a sphere of her own, shaping her own vision of the ministry and acting on that vision once it has been approved by her senior pastor. She meets biweekly with the senior pastor to establish outcomes and align her focus with his, but those meetings seldom result in sudden priority shifts. Libby's senior pastor wouldn't presume to direct Libby in how to do her job. Libby knows far more about faith formation and discipleship than the senior pastor is ever likely to know, and both she and the senior pastor understand this.

Libby doesn't share the same sense of role confusion that Audrey reports. The boundaries of Libby's role are firmly established, and she understands where her authority begins and ends. Libby's greatest challenge lies in figuring out how to shape the direction of her ministry and how to garner support for her initiatives without having regular access to the pulpit and without full access to the governing board. She doesn't sit on the governing board and only attends meetings at the invitation of the senior pastor. She often feels that her ministry area gets shortchanged in the operating budget, and she has little voice in budget allocation decisions. The senior pastor is always willing to represent Libby's ministry from the pulpit and in board meetings, but representation is not the same as being able to share her aspirations directly. These limitations of the role sometimes result in Libby feeling disempowered in the larger congregational system.

There are times when the strategic vision of the senior minister doesn't seem large enough to hold Libby's vision. She sees some things that the senior minister is missing. Although she doesn't want the senior minister's job, she does think at times that she could do the job better, particularly with regard to oversight of her ministry area.

The Right Fit

Libby and Audrey face different organizational challenges by virtue of the fact that they minister to different size congregations. It is clear that somewhere between the 375 and 850 weekly worship attendance number, three significant shifts occur in the role of the associate pastor. The shift is gradual and unique to each ministry context, but clearly observable—from a developmental pass-through role to a vocational role, from a generalist orientation to a specialist orientation, and from porous role boundaries to firmer role boundaries. When very large congregations do not accommodate these shifts in the associate role, they are likely to experience misfit problems between staff member and congregation.

The "newly corporate" congregation that narrowly defines an associate ministry role as a specialist role is likely to discover that it does not have a large enough staff team to accommodate specialization. The person who accepts a role in this church expecting to operate as a specialist will become resentful, because others continually want to relax the boundaries of the role and pile on responsibilities well outside the scope of the defined ministry specialty. On the church's side, resentments emerge because the associate seems resistant to chipping in and helping out as needed in all areas of ministry.

Similarly, if the very large congregation mistakenly structures an associate ministry role as a generalist position, it also frustrates itself and its minister. The work of the generalist associate will be compared to the work of other associates with more specialized ministries, and the generalist's performance will be labeled substandard. People will look for specific areas of excellence and will register their disappointment that the associate is neither as good a generalist as the senior minister nor demonstrating the kind of program brilliance that they see from other specialists on the team.

Creating a healthy associate pastor role requires clarity about the impact of congregational size on role definition. Both congregation and minister must be clear about the suitability of generalist versus specialist role expectations. They must have clarity about the developmental versus vocational nature of the position and the type of oversight that will accompany the role. Finally, they must specify whether the position will operate with firm or porous boundaries.

THE EXECUTIVE CLERGY ROLE

In *When Moses Meets Aaron: Staffing and Supervision in Large Congregations,* my colleague Gil Rendle wrote about the distinction between those who manage and those who lead in the large church:

A Jewish midrash speaks of Moses as the voice of leadership for the Israelites. It was Moses who went apart to speak with God and who returned with a glowing face and new insight in the future of God's people. Aaron was the voice of management to complement Moses' leadership. It was Aaron who organized the journey and met the more immediate needs of the people. The midrash points out that it is essential but not sufficient simply to provide both leadership and management. Of equal importance is keeping leadership and management connected and aligned. When Moses was on top of the mountain receiving the commandments, he was separated by too much distance from Aaron, who was at that very moment at the base of the mountain breaking one of the commandments. While casting an idol seemed expedient to Aaron, it was in opposition to the vision Moses receive of being a people who were faithful to the one true God. If the first lesson was sharing leadership, the second lesson was about alignment and connections.[4]

The alignment of leadership and management is a key challenge for the large congregation. In the small to mid-sized congregation, leadership and management are naturally aligned in the role of the pastor. The solo or lead pastor discerns the vision, articulates the vision, and translates the vision into actionable ministry in the congregation. Once the congregation passes beyond the multi-celled size category and into the professional size zone, it is no longer possible for one person to provide full oversight of both the leadership and management functions. At this point, Moses needs an Aaron.

In the professional size congregation, the first Aaron who emerges is a middle manager who tends to the administrative side of church life. A business administrator (or some equivalent) takes supervisory responsibility for all of those employees who tend to the facility, accounting, finance, communications, and reception functions. This frees the senior clergy leader to oversee these functions and allows her to focus more fully on the worship, program, and care life of the congregation. This arrangement keeps the professional size congregation in alignment, provided that a good performance-management system is put in place to ensure clear expectations and feedback.[5]

Somewhere in the strategic size category, the worship, programmatic, and care staff team becomes too large for the senior clergy leader to effectively supervise. (See chapter 5, "Staff Team Design and Function.") Staff members begin to feel that they are operating without adequate supervision and that the various ministries of the congregation are out of alignment. Senior staff leaders realize that they have too many direct reports and that another level of management is needed in the life of the congregation. At this moment large congregations have several options for restoring alignment. One option is to appoint several higher-level directors to oversee cluster areas of program ministry. For example, one of the associate pastors may become an executive associate pastor in charge of discipleship, taking responsibility for all of children's ministry, youth ministry, and adult ministry. She may have several pastors reporting to her. This collective leadership body will function as a discrete team. Another pastor or director may be appointed to oversee all of the member care functions of the congregation (including pastoral care, membership, weddings, and funerals). A third pastor or director is appointed to oversee the department of music and worship. The clustering of supervisory relationships in this manner reduces the number of direct reports the senior clergy leader must maintain. (See chapter 5 for more information on how this clustering feature works in the design of the staff team.) The role of the senior clergy leader becomes more about aligning segments of the team and less about the day-to-day management of those teams.

At some point, typically toward the higher end of the strategic size category, it becomes apparent to everyone that the senior clergy leader needs to be spending more time on things other than staff team supervision. More time needs to be invested in preaching, writing, board development, fundraising, and community and denominational presence. At the same time programmatic staff team members begin to feel that they are not receiving enough guidance in their respective areas of ministry. Fiefdoms are emerging and turf wars are developing as various segments of the staff team vie for congregational resources.

This is often the moment when a full-blown executive clergy role emerges in the congregation. In some instances the executive clergy leader oversees the entire staff team, including the church business administrator. In other instances the church business administrator continues to report to the senior clergy person, and the executive minister provides oversight for the entire worship, programmatic, and care side of the staff team. This arrangement reduces the number of direct reports to the senior clergy leader to one or two individuals. In either case, the senior clergy leader, the executive pastor, and the church business administrator typically form an executive leadership team that ensures the alignment of leadership and management.

Core Competencies of the Executive Pastor (EP)

When a large congregation hires an executive pastor, the strategic leadership of the church is divided into two parts. The senior clergy leader takes responsibility for vision and strategic leadership. It is the role of senior clergy to discern and establish a clear, achievable and compelling vision and core purpose; articulate possibilities; reflect optimism; create mileposts and symbols to rally support behind the vision; and make the vision sharable by everyone. The executive clergy leader takes responsibility for the execution of strategy. The executive clergy leader is future oriented but focuses on church operation. The executive pastor focuses on managing the plan and vision.

In many ways the core competencies of an executive pastor and the senior clergy leader overlap. The executive clergy leader does not carry the preaching and fundraising responsibilities that the senior clergy leader shoulders. Consequently, the executive pastor does not need the same level of competence in speaking, preaching, and projecting a public presence. The executive pastor does need strengths in other areas that may no longer be particularly important for the senior clergy leader to possess. Below you'll find my "top ten" list of competencies needed in the executive pastor role. This list is meant to be descriptive of the administrative side of the role and doesn't address any teaching or pastoral responsibilities that an executive pastor may have.

1. **Conflict Management Skills:** Understands the dynamics of human negotiation among conflicting interest groups and how to achieve mutual agreement; steps up to conflicts, seeing them as opportunities; reads situations quickly; finds common ground and gets cooperation with minimum anxiety.
2. **Negotiation Skills:** Can negotiate skillfully in tough situations with both internal and external groups; can settle

differences with minimal conflict; can win concessions without damaging relationships; can be direct and forceful as well as diplomatic; quickly gains trust of other parties to the negotiations.

3. **Organizational Agility**: Knowledgeable about how the congregation works; knows how to get things done both through formal channels and informal networks; can maneuver through complex political situations effectively and astutely; anticipates where the organizational barriers are and plans her approach accordingly.

4. **Problem-Solving Skills**: Uses sound logic and analysis to approach difficult problems and apply effective solutions; can distinguish between symptoms, causes, and implied solutions; decides in a timely manner based upon a mixture of analysis, wisdom, experience, and judgment.

5. **Priority-Setting Ability**: Spends her time and the time of others on what's important; quickly zeros in on the critical few and puts the trivial many aside; can quickly sense what will help or hinder in accomplishing a goal; eliminates roadblocks; projects a clear focus.

6. **Project Management Skills**: Identifies key objectives and scope of a proposed project; garners needed resources and project support; develops a realistic and thorough plan for achieving key objectives; keeps team members briefed on progress; implements action plans; communicates progress to sponsors; identifies barriers and resolves problems.

7. **Team-Building Orientation**: Demonstrates interest, skill, and success in team environments; places group goals ahead of personal agendas; offers self as a resource to other members of the team; shares credit for success with others.

8. **Hiring and Staffing Skills**: Identifies new talent; hires the best people available from inside or outside the organization; is not afraid of selecting strong people; does not discriminate in hiring practices.

9. **Motivation Skills**: Creates a climate in which people want to do their best; can motivate individuals, team, or project members, even those individuals who do not report directly to her; empowers others; invites shared input and

decision making; makes each individual feel that her work is important.

10. **Supervisory Skills:** Is good at establishing clear expectations and setting clear direction; sets stretching objectives; distributes the workload appropriately; provides regular and ongoing feedback about performance; proactively deals with substandard performance; engages disciplinary processes in a timely manner.

A question that frequently emerges when a congregation is considering adding an executive pastor is whether the occupant of the role needs to have theological training and ordination status. In 2009 the Leadership Network conducted a comprehensive survey about the role of the executive pastor. Responses were drawn from 555 executive pastors serving in congregations where weekly attendance ranged from 100 to 23,000. Nearly one-third of responders (28 percent) indicated they had had no theological training. Meanwhile, 70 percent indicated they had spent at least five years in a non-church field, with "business" ranking much higher than "education," "military," or "other." Among those who did have theological training, 34 percent indicated they held a master's degree, and another 12 percent said they had a degree from a Bible college.[6] It appears that most executive pastors have theological training, but most have also acquired their managerial skills in non-church arenas.

Time Management

Those executive pastors who possess theological training and are ordained almost always have responsibilities that involve worship, teaching, and pastoral care. Time management pressure is more palpable for ordained clergy in executive roles, as they struggle to balance their pastoral and administrative responsibilities. Those individuals without a theological orientation are more inclined to define the role as purely administrative in nature and may in fact experience less role conflict. Nevertheless, many congregations believe it is critical for someone in a leadership position of this significance to have some kind of theological training. If the executive pastor oversees other ordained staff, then the EP is almost always an ordained person, as most ordained clergy balk at being supervised by someone who is not also ordained.

The Leadership Network survey mentioned above also assessed how EPs spend their time. On average, executive pastors' report spending the majority of their time in three areas: supervising staff (46 percent), doing administrative tasks (32 percent), and making budget decisions (24 percent). These findings are highly consistent with what I have observed in my own practice.

Leading Up

The executive pastor faces challenges that are unique compared with any other leadership role in the congregation. He needs to serve as head of staff and also needs to guide the work of the board without being fully in charge of either. The authority of the executive pastor is always subject to reversal at the whim of the senior clergy leader. This requires having vision without being the one who gets to set the vision. It requires setting a clear direction but being open to having the senior clergy leader change that direction. At times it requires pulling the vision out of a senior clergy leader who hasn't done a particularly good job of articulating it. In short, the executive pastor needs to be skilled at leading upward.

In his book *Leading Up,* author Michael Useem discusses upward leadership as the effective exercise of power for the greater good. Leading up is not a call for undermining authority or seizing power. The challenge is to help both those above and below you in the organizational structure achieve what you all want accomplished. Leading up can require enormous fortitude, perseverance, and courage.[7]

Likewise, for the senior clergy leader, receiving upward leadership—a willingness to be led even when you are "the one in charge"—is a learned competency. The senior clergy leader who fails to fully honor the visionary insights of an executive pastor has lost an important congregational resource.

The roles that clergy leaders assume in the life of the congregation are always in a state of flux. They change as the missional priorities of the congregation change; they change with fluctuations in attendance and budget size. Like all the other leadership systems of the church, the roles of clergy must be managed with insight and care. A change in the role of one leader on the team has far reaching implications for every other member of the team. The large congregation will make the best use of its clergy resources if church leaders are careful to clearly articulate expectations around core competencies and essential functions.

QUESTIONS FOR INDIVIDUAL OR GROUP REFLECTION

1. What is the history of your congregation's expectations about the senior clergy role? In what ways has the role evolved over the years? How have various senior ministers played the role? Which congregational expectations of the senior clergy leader have endured over time? Are those expectations appropriate or inappropriate, given the size of your congregation?

2. What are the essential functions that your congregation expects the senior minister to fulfill? What are the core competencies that your congregation expects the senior minister to demonstrate? Are these appropriate expectations? If not, which expectations need to change?

3. What kind of expectations does your congregation carry about the role that clergy spouses and families should play in the life of the congregation? What kind of stress are these expectations placing upon the families of your clergy leaders?

4. When you consider the associate clergy roles in your congregation, would you describe those roles as generalist or specialist positions? In what ways does the orientation as a specialist or generalist create tension for the occupants of those roles?

5. Are your associate clergy on a developmental pass-through career track (accumulating experience in your congregation before they move on to serve as senior pastors in congregations of their own), or are they serving in their preferred area of specialty? What kinds of expectations does the congregation carry with regard to this question?

6. Does your congregation operate with an executive pastor role (or equivalent role)? If not, are you large enough to support this kind of role? How will you know (what symptoms will you see) when the congregation is ready for that kind of role?

INDIVIDUAL EXERCISE: ROLE CONFLICT

Role conflict is a condition that occurs when competing expectations about a role cannot be mutually satisfied. Role conflict is a common condition among clergy in congregations that are not appropriately staffed and structured. Different parts of the congregational system operate with competing expectations about the role, and the occupant of the role cannot find a way to satisfy the competing demands.

The first step in dealing with role conflict is to clearly name the competing expectations placed upon the role. Once the competing expectations have been identified, the occupant of the role and congregational leaders can begin negotiating a more appropriately boundaried role.

1. Spend some time with the diagram on the next page. Jot notes in each box indicating what you currently know about the expectations that each of the following entities have about the role being examined:
   • The governing board
   • Other members of the staff team
   • The individual's supervisor

- The constituency that the role serves
- The occupant of the role

2. Under the heading "Enacted Role," make some notes about how the occupant of the role has reconciled the competing expectations into a cohesive set of behaviors that he or she plays out on a daily basis.

3. Is the presence and source of role conflict becoming clearer in your own mind? Are the expectations that others are placing on the role appropriate for the size and complexity of your congregation? How many hours per week would the individual in the role need to work to satisfy all of the expectations that exist? What steps can you take to rightsize the expectations of others? What steps can you take to rightsize your own expectations? How would the expectations around a role be different if the congregation was acting more appropriately for its size?

Figure 4.1   Where Is Your Role Conflict Coming From?

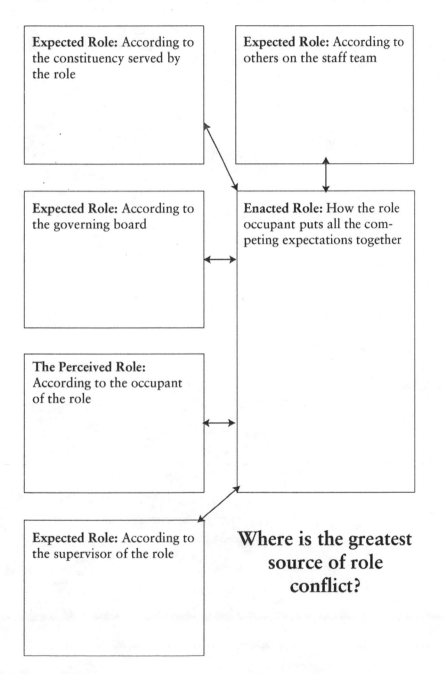

Expected Role: According to the constituency served by the role

Expected Role: According to others on the staff team

Expected Role: According to the governing board

Enacted Role: How the role occupant puts all the competing expectations together

The Perceived Role: According to the occupant of the role

Expected Role: According to the supervisor of the role

Where is the greatest source of role conflict?

CHAPTER 5

Staff Team Design and Function

HOW THEN SHALL WE ORGANIZE THE WORK OF THE CHURCH AND ITS leaders? For centuries the church has been asking itself this question and looking to Scripture for answers. Back in chapter 2, we listened in on a conversation between Moses and his father-in-law, Jethro, as they talked about an organizing scheme that would establish leadership authority and divide responsibility among the exiled Israelites, so the leadership burden on Moses would be lessened. In Numbers we encounter the appointment of the Levites as the priestly tribe that will tend to the ritual needs of the community. We also read about the gathering and appointment of 70 elders, upon whom the Spirit of God rests as they lead. From the beginning, the challenges inherent in organizing people for ministry have been evident.

In the first generation of the Christian church, the issue of organizational design emerges in Acts 6. A conflict between the Hellenists and the Hebrews produces awareness that the skill of preachers and teachers is not ideally suited to tending the community's food-management system. By the time we arrive at Acts 11, we see the church struggling with leadership needs in newly formed faith communities, and Barnabus is appointed to go and serve these nascent communities. He selects Saul to serve with him, and the first co-pastorate is born (not without its own share of problems). By the fifteenth chapter of Acts a potential schism in

111

the church has given rise to the first executive team, a body of leaders designated to oversee the work of other leaders.

Questions about how to organize the workers who organize the work of others have always been with us. Today, the questions are expressed differently, but they are fundamentally the same questions found in Acts. What is the real role of a staff team? Are they doers of the ministry, or do they exist to organize the doers of the ministry? How many ordained clergy leaders do you need in any given sized congregation? What is the appropriate relationship between programmatic leadership and administrative leadership in a congregation? How large is big enough; that is, how large a staff team is needed to effectively lead various size congregations? What is the role of volunteerism on a staff team? How much of our operating budget should be devoted to payroll-related expenses? How should the supervisory relationships in a congregation be organized? What is the role of an executive team in the large congregation? All these questions regularly emerge in my practice with large congregations.

This chapter addresses the fundamental questions that surround staff team size and design in the large congregation, not managing or supervising the performance of a staff team. For a more in-depth treatment of supervision, the reader is directed to *When Moses Meets Aaron: Staffing and Supervision in the Large Congregation* by Gil Rendle and Susan Beaumont.

WHO IS STAFF?

Karen is a 15-year member of Shady Valley Methodist Church. She raised her children in the church, but they are all out of the house now, and Karen has some significant time available that she would like to devote to volunteer work at the church. Karen has a passion for youth ministry. For the past five years Karen has been volunteering 10 to 15 hours a week, providing administrative support to the youth minister. Is Karen a member of the staff team?

Kaysar is on the payroll of Mason Community Church. He works five to seven hours a week tending the grounds of the church.

Kaysar schedules his hours to fit the demands of his class schedule at the university. Kaysar is not a member of the congregation and has no particular investment in the mission of the congregation. Is Kaysar a member of the staff team?

Before we can begin talking about the appropriate size of a staff team, we need to get clear on what we mean when we use the term *staff team*. Who is staff? The question seems almost too obvious, doesn't it? When asked this question, most church leaders respond that the staff of the church is the group of people the church employs. And that response is more or less accurate. However, many congregations have volunteers who effectively serve as staff members of the church and don't get paid anything—volunteers who devote significant, dedicated, and predictable hours in service to the congregation and do not expect or accept compensation for what they do. Churches also employ some very part-time employees who are only minimally tied to the missional outcomes of the congregation (e.g., a part-time landscape worker) who don't really function as members of the staff team.

So what is staff, and what role does it play in the large church? Dictionary.com provides this definition of *staff*. "Staff (noun): a group of persons, as employees, charged with carrying out the work of an establishment, or executing some undertaking on its behalf."[1] Many church leaders assume this rather secular definition with regard to their staff teams. The staff is here to engage in ministry on our behalf. The problem with this definition is that the staff team of a congregation does not undertake the work of ministry in place of the congregation; it exists to equip the laity in pursuit of the congregation's mission. When a staff team and its leaders confuse the difference between the work of the laity and the work that is theirs to do, the congregation is less impactful. A staff team of 25 cannot accomplish what a congregation of 800 can accomplish within a community. The staff team works in service to the mission and on behalf of the congregation but does not carry out the work of the congregation. The work of the congregation always belongs to the laity.

Some congregations become very fearful about the staff team taking away work that legitimately belongs to the laity. A definition of staff that may work its way into the psyche of these congregations is more along the lines of the military definition of staff. "A group of officers without command authority, appointed to assist a commanding officer; or the parts of any army concerned with administrative matters, planning, etc., rather than with actual participation in combat."[2] If we eliminate the references to army and combat, we actually have a pretty good working definition of how some congregations view their staff. The staff is here to administer and execute the ministry that the boards and committees of the church craft for them to do. The laity strategizes and plans, and the staff executes. The problem with this orientation is that it keeps staff out of the critical planning and decision-making conversations, ultimately limiting their ministry impact.

Consider instead this working definition of staff, as an alternative to the secular and military definitions:

> The staff of a congregation exists to organize the human, financial, and capital resources of the congregation, in pursuit of the congregation's mission. Staff are those individuals, paid and unpaid, who commit to working regularly scheduled hours and agree to be subject to ongoing supervision. They are able to claim some attachment to the mission of the congregation.

This definition allows for the use of volunteer staff, those willing to work without pay and willing to subject themselves to the accountability systems of a staff team (i.e., job description, performance evaluations, supervisory relationships, and participation in staff team meetings). The definition also helps to distinguish between staff members who are committed to the missional outcomes of the congregation and those part-time contract employees for whom there are no missional expectations. (I would argue that these employees are not actually staff.) Furthermore, this definition empowers members of the staff to participate freely and fully in the decision making of the congregation, provided that their participation serves the congregation's mission.

Volunteers Who Serve as Staff

At some point every large church asks the question, "Are we utilizing volunteers the way we should?" The question usually emerges in the midst of a budgeting or financial planning meeting as leaders grapple with an ever-expanding staff budget or yet another request for an addition to staff. It seems volunteers ought to be able to substitute for some of the hired staff of the congregation. Sometimes the question emerges in a board meeting as lay leaders try to figure out what the role of laity is in a congregation where the staff team seems to be coordinating the work of the congregation. What, if any, meaningful role do lay volunteers play within the large staff-driven congregation?

Once a congregation passes a certain size threshold, the complexity of running the church requires an organizational structure that centers on a professional staff team. After a congregation passes 450-500 people in weekend worship attendance or functions with an operating budget of more than $1 million, the congregation begins to operate with standards of excellence in programming and worship that are almost impossible to maintain solely with volunteer leadership. It's not that lay leaders don't have the desire or ability to create excellent programs; it's that they don't have the time or expertise. Beyond a certain point, excellence requires consistent and regular hours and expertise in a particular area of ministry. Once a congregation passes this threshold, laity often struggle to understand their part in the ministry.

In the large church the relationship between staff and lay leaders can be characterized in these simple terms. Lay leadership is responsible for the *governance* (policy making, oversight, accountability) of church life. The staff team is responsible for *management* (program leadership and daily administration) of the church. Together, lay and staff leadership have shared responsibility for mission, vision, and strategy. For a better understanding of these distinctions and this relationship, see chapter 6, "Governance and Board Function."

Having made these distinctions, let's explore the role of volunteerism in both governance and ministry. In congregational life the governance work is an entirely volunteer process. The work of governance is carried out by the governing body and its appointed committees, all volunteer operating groups. The work of ministry is managed by the professional staff team of the church and lay volunteers who serve on committees that help to shape and support those ministries. Volunteers also function as ministry participants (choir members, teachers, youth workers, mission project participants, and the like).

When congregations begin to wonder if there isn't a better way to utilize volunteers to reduce staffing costs, they typically aren't thinking about adding more volunteers on the governance side of the equation, and they typically aren't thinking about adding more volunteers as ministry participants. They are most often thinking about using volunteers in the management and administration of ministry.

So, what is the correct way to think about utilizing volunteers in the management and administration of ministry? Simply put, volunteerism on the staff team can work if the volunteer is:

- Equipped with all of the skills required to fulfill the role. The large church can't operate with multiple semi-equipped volunteers in a role that needs the devoted skill of a professional. Willingness to help and the availability of time cannot substitute for expertise.
- Committed to keeping regular and consistent hours. Volunteers who have isolated pockets of time and are looking to work only when it's convenient for them don't work well as volunteers in the large congregation. Volunteer staff must schedule and coordinate their time away from the job just like paid staff members do.
- Willing to be subject to accountability standards. Staff volunteers need to function with defined job descriptions, participate in regular supervisory meetings, and receive regular performance feedback, including annual reviews.

When these three sets of conditions are met, volunteers can and do function effectively as members of a staff team.

How Large Is Big Enough?

Meadowbrook Presbyterian Church is in the midst of a staffing assessment. Leaders have decided it is time to do an in-depth analysis of the staff team to determine if it is the right size and appropriately configured to serve the new strategic plan. The personnel committee has gathered with several members of the session, the senior pastor, and the church consultant to talk about their hopes for the assessment and their concerns about the present structure.

As the dialogue opens, it quickly becomes apparent that leaders have some high-level concern about the percentage of the operating budget that is devoted to salary and benefits. Leaders begin to tell the story about the glory days of the church (back in the 1960s) when the congregation sent half of its annual operating budget to local and overseas mission. As leaders talk about the congregation's historic commitment to a 50/50 split of the operating budget, it becomes clear that many still think of this as an attainable ideal. "If we get healthy and all is right with the world again, we should be able to get back to this number."

Today, Meadowbrook's membership and attendance are about half of what they were back in those glory days. Payroll expense consumes 53 percent of the operating budget, and missional support has been reduced to 15 percent. The staff team has already been through two significant downsizings in the past five years, but the church has not eliminated any programming or ministry in those years. Each reduction in staff has carried with it the expectation that existing staff will somehow carry on, and staff members are exhausted. At the end of the day, everyone wants to know, "How many staff do we really need to run a congregation of this size, and how much should it cost us? Are the old ideals we cling to even attainable anymore?"

Many factors influence the size of a staff team. Among these are attendance, the size of the operating budget, growth or decline rate, affluence of the community, geographical location, denominational affiliation, and the age of the church. The first two factors, attendance and operating budget, are the two factors most frequently cited when people talk about the size of a staff team. Specifically, how many paid staff do we need given the size of our active membership (typically represented by average weekend worship attendance)? And what percentage of our budget should be dedicated to payroll-related expenses?

Percentage of Operating Budget

Faith Communities Today (Fact 2008) is a study that looked at, among other things, how 3,000 congregations allocated their budgets.[3] Researchers discovered that the average U.S. Protestant congregation allocates 45 percent of its total operating budget to payroll-related costs. Mainline churches spend considerably more (49 percent) on payroll-related expenses than either the Evangelical Protestant (31 percent) or the Catholic/Orthodox communities (41 percent).

Intuitively, most of us expect that the larger a congregation becomes, the smaller that payroll expense will be relative to the overall operating budget. We expect some economies of scale to exist. In fact, research does not support the notion of economies of scale in the size range covered by this text (400–2,000 in worship attendance.)

A 2010 study conducted by Warren Bird of the Leadership Network on lean staffing structures examined how the percentage of operating budget dedicated to salary changed relative to a variety of factors, including size.[4] The study revealed that staff costs do become leaner as overall weekend worship attendance increases but not dramatically and not until the congregation passes the 5,000 mark in weekend worship attendance.

Attendance	Staff Costs as a Percentage of Budget
500	48 percent
1000	50 percent
1500	46 percent
2000	46 percent
3000	46 percent
4000	47 percent
6000	42 percent
10000	42 percent

The Leadership Network study found that the following factors were somewhat related to staff costs:

- Whether the church is growing. Staffing costs are leaner for churches whose attendance is growing, perhaps because growing churches have not "caught up" with additional staffing needs.
- The dominant age group of the congregation. Staffing costs are leaner, but only slightly, for churches where the average person's age in the congregation is lower.
- The year in which the church was founded. The younger the church, the leaner the staffing costs.
- The location of the church. Staffing costs are lower for residential and new suburban locations and slightly higher for older suburb and downtown churches.
- Race. Staffing costs are leanest for predominantly African American churches and highest for Anglo-European churches.
- Use of paid part-time staff. Staffing costs have no relationship to the percentage of paid part-time staff in relation to full-time staff until a congregation employs three or more paid part-timers for each full-time staff member.
- Economic level of the congregation. Staffing costs are leanest for churches whose internal constituency is described as poor and highest for churches with an internal constituency described as wealthy.

Staffing/Membership Ratios

Perhaps the longest standing rule of thumb about staffing structures is the ratio of program staff to average worship attendance. In 1965 Martin Anderson wrote one of the first books to address staffing models in the larger church. He recommended a staffing ratio of 1 pastor for every 500 *members* (1:500).[5] Looking back on that number, it is hard to believe that congregations ever functioned with such lean staff teams, but in fact they did. Remember that Anderson's book was written during a time when worship attendance and membership were more closely aligned, when membership meant different things than it does today, when volunteerism in the church worked differently, and when church programming was more homogenous and standardized than it is today. No church today would ever dream of targeting a 1:500 staffing ratio and expect to meet the needs of its congregants.

In 1980 Lyle Schaller wrote *The Multiple Staff and the Larger Church* in which he introduced average worship attendance as a more reliable indicator of staffing needs. Schaller proposed a ratio of 1:100 as a guideline for the typical ratio of full-time paid professional staff positions in mainline Protestant congregations.[6] In 2000 Gary McIntosh wrote *Staff Your Church for Growth* and suggested that a 1:150 paid professional staff ratio was a more realistic and affordable guideline.[7] Both Schaller and McIntosh focused on the combination of professional clergy leaders and professional program staff leaders. Their ratios did not include administrative or support staff. Both assumed that the staffing ratio remained constant across size ranges.

So, given these conflicting guidelines, what is the most effective way to think about the size of the staff team relative to the active membership base of the congregation? The same 2010 Leadership Network Study that looked at the characteristics of a lean staff team created an alternative way of thinking about staff size relative to attendance. Rather than thinking solely about program or clergy staff in relationship to attendance, the Leadership Network study looked at the ratio of *all* full-time staff equivalents (FTEs) to attendance. Furthermore, the study looked at how that ratio changed as the percentage of budget devoted to staffing expense increased and decreased. Here is what they found:

Staff Costs as a Percentage of Budget	Ratio of Staff to Attendees
10-19%	1:108
20-29%	1:91
30-39%	1:73
40-49%	1:73
50-59%	1:70
60-69%	1:59

The conclusion here is obvious. If you spend more of your budget on staff, then you have more staff per attendee than other congregations do. The results also suggest that churches with higher staffing budgets don't necessarily pay their staff better; they just hire more staff. The ratios are helpful benchmarks as to how many staff congregations employ. Given that the average large congregation spends between 48 and 50 percent of its operating budget on payroll, we can assume the average large congregation employs one full-time equivalent staff member for every 70 to 73 people in average weekend worship attendance.

The Balance between Clergy, Program, and Support Staff

Congregations don't simply want to know how many staff to hire. They also want to know what the balance should be between clergy, program staff, and support staff. Unable to locate any solid research that addresses this particular question, I decided to do some data gathering from my own client base. Over the course of three years, I collected information on the staffing structures of 83 different congregations in a variety of mainline Protestant traditions. Most of the data was gathered from pastors who attended Alban educational events related to the large church. Some of the data comes from congregations that I worked with more closely in a consulting capacity. Willing pastors/congregations were asked to provide:

- Annual operating budget of the congregation
- Average weekend attendance
- Number of clergy FTEs (full-time equivalents)
- Number of program staff FTEs
- Number of administrative staff FTEs
- A diagram of how the staff team was structured (including position titles and reporting relationships)

It is important to note that none of the data provided was audited or verified. Because most of the data was gathered in retreat settings, the data providers were seldom consulting actual financial data as they completed the provided worksheet. Participants were simply offering their best approximations of what had been happening in their own contexts, using their own definitions of average weekly attendance, and their own definitions of program and support staff. There are undoubtedly errors in the data with this methodology.

It is also important to note that there was no attempt to distinguish between thriving, stagnant, or declining congregations. This data cannot be used to make generalizations about the features of healthy verses dysfunctional congregations. The data simply illustrate normative behavior in Alban's client base. The data included in this informal study came from congregations ranging in size from average weekend attendance of 170 to 1300. The congregations reported annual operating budgets ranging from $175,000 to $4,400,000.

When sorted according to average worship attendance, the data yielded interesting insights into how the composition of the staff team shifts as the congregation grows.

Average Worship	Clergy FTE	Program Staff FTE	Admin Support FTE
200-399	2.2	1.9	2.3
400-599	2.5	3.0	3.4
600-799	3.0	5.6	3.7
800-999	2.5	6.3	11.0
1,000-1,199	5.4	7.0	12.7

It is difficult to make generalizations about how many clergy it takes to effectively serve the large congregation. Congregations embrace a wide diversity of practices. Most congregations have added a second clergyperson to the staff by the time average worship attendance reaches 250, and a third clergyperson by the time average worship attendance reaches 500. However, there were congregations in our sample that served worshiping communities of over 800 with only two clergy staff. The employment of clergy staff seems more closely related to budget size than attendance patterns. Also, denominational affiliation seems to have a bigger impact on size of the clergy staff than do attendance patterns.

Denominational traditions hold different expectations regarding the role of clergy and laity in preaching, and the administration of sacraments. Those traditions that invest only clergy with these responsibilities tend to have larger clergy staffs, with correspondingly smaller program staff teams.

The program staff is made up of those who directly oversee the development and maintenance of worship, music, congregational care, education, membership, service, and outreach ministries of the congregation; in other words, those ministries that tend to be programmatic in nature. This component of the staff team grows consistently and steadily as the size of the congregation grows. Continued growth of the congregation requires continual expansion of programming. Predictably, program staff positions become increasingly specialized as the congregation grows, and additional staff is required to accommodate the increasing demands of the congregation.

The administrative staff is made up of those who support the operational side of church life, including reception, building maintenance, accounting/finance, personnel, communication, information technology, and general administrative support. The administrative side of the staff team grows slowly in comparison to the program team until average worship reaches 800. Upon reaching this threshold, the administrative team begins growing more quickly than either the clergy or program staff. The programs of the congregation can continue growing in size only if there is adequate support to track the people participating in the life of the congregation, enough staff to support the increased usage of the building, and sufficient staff to ensure effective communication and accounting.

In a congregation with average worship attendance of 200–400 (the multi-celled congregation), the staff team is fairly balanced between clergy staff, program staff, and administrative staff. When average worship attendance is 400–800 (the professional church), most of the growth on the staff team occurs through the addition of program staff. This component of the staff team becomes larger than either the clergy or administrative staff. In the strategic church (800-1,200), there is still some growth in both clergy and program staff, but the vast majority of growth is seen in the addition of administrative staff. The administrative team becomes significantly larger than either the clergy or program staff.

HOW SHOULD THE TEAM BE ORGANIZED?

At the core of every organizational design for a staff team are four basic questions that must be resolved:

1. How will work be divided up? (Division of Labor)
2. How will we integrate and coordinate the work? (Integrating Mechanisms)
3. At what level of the organization will decisions be made? (Centralization)
4. How many employees will report to a single manager or supervisor? (Span of Control)

Let us begin by better understanding the questions. Then we can move on to explore how different size congregations answer these questions, producing significantly different staffing structures.

Division of Labor

How do we divide up the work of the staff team, so the right people are engaged in the right kinds of tasks? This is the essence of the division-of-labor problem. A staff member working in a small to mid-size congregation is accustomed to working as a generalist. If there is a task to be done, the person who becomes aware of the need is often the person who completes the task. Some members of the team are specialists, particularly in the area of music ministry, but most function as generalists. In the large congregation the whole staff team is specialized. While the team as a whole may still function with a collaborative spirit, where everyone helps out as needed, most members of the team have a specialty. Specialization means that staff members are hired for their giftedness in particular ministry areas (teaching, pastoral care, small groups, young adults, communication), and they are expected to spend the majority of their time engaged in those specialties. The large church doesn't work well when the division of labor doesn't honor specialization.

Recently I consulted with a congregation in which every member of the staff team was eager, willing, and able to help every other member of the team as needed. Staff members had their areas of specialty, but there were no boundaries between the more relational/spiritual work of some staff members and the more administrative tasks of others. When interviewed individually, staff members were asked to speak about what they were responsible for and where the boundaries of their roles began and ended. Every member of the staff team could define the center of his or her particular area of ministry ("I am responsible for youth ministry"), but individual roles didn't seem to have any firm boundaries. Over and over again I was told, "I help out with everything. There isn't anything that is not part of my role."

At first I found myself incredibly drawn to this team. They operated with a wonderful spirit of camaraderie. Everyone supported everyone else all of the time. No one bad-mouthed any other member of the team. As I spent more time with the team, however, I began to notice several disturbing phenomena. Staff members collectively reported spending more than a third of their time interfacing with one another. It takes time to be highly collaborative, and this team began to realize that they were sometimes investing in relationships with one another to the detriment of their individual ministries and their focus on the congregation. It also became evident, as I watched this team, that their boundaries with one another were so porous that individual performance management was virtually nonexistent. In other words, people helped one another so frequently that it had become impossible to identify poor performers and hold them accountable for problems in their areas of responsibility. This staff team seemed particularly exhausted to me. With no solid division of labor, everyone was responsible for everything, and team members ran themselves ragged trying to maintain excellence in every area of ministry, not just their own.

Division of labor in the large congregation requires clarity about the essential functions of each role, those duties and tasks unique to each job. Good division of labor requires the jobs have clearly defined boundaries, so each member of the team is empowered to say, "I'm sorry, I'm not the best person to address that issue, but I can direct you to the person best equipped to address your request."

Integrating Mechanisms

How will we coordinate the work we do? The division of labor only works well if integrating mechanisms built into a staff structure allow the team to coordinate its work. In the small congregation, integrating mechanisms aren't particularly important because the staff team simply isn't big enough to require formal coordination. The process of supervision can be used by the pastor to coordinate decision making and communication with other staff members (if there are other staff members).

In the mid-sized congregation integration happens pretty naturally in the staff team meeting. The staff team, including key volunteers, meets weekly to make decisions and to coordinate shared work. If coordination is needed outside the staff team, it is pretty easy for staff members to connect in a hallway or over coffee to keep things on track.

The larger the staff team becomes, the greater the complexity involved in communication and decision making. Once the staff team exceeds seven people, its capacity for group decision making begins to diminish significantly. Staff team meetings become long and tedious reporting sessions with minimal effective decision making taking place. (See chapter 2, "How Size Changes Things.") Eventually the staff team needs to reorganize into a structure that allows for smaller coordinating and decision-making bodies to emerge. An education department forms. The music ministry group begins having its own staff meetings. The administrative staff team members discover that they need to meet as a team, without the program staff present, to work through some of the nuts-and-bolts issues that they face as administrators. The full staff team still finds the need to meet together, but less often and for different purposes. The all-staff meeting becomes less about coordination and decision making and more about morale building and vision casting.

In general, as size and complexity increase, integrating and co-ordinating mechanisms need to be more carefully defined. Team members still rely on hallway conversations and meeting over a cup of coffee to coordinate their work, but the collective team develops a more tightly structured set of subgroups within which work gets accomplished.

Centralization

At what level of the organization will decisions be made? We already began the discussion about decision making when we posed the question about integration and coordination. Here we continue the conversation through the lens of centralization (kept close to the head of staff) or decentralization (dispersed widely throughout the team). For example, decision making about worship tends to be centralized in most large congregations. The head of staff and a few others generally make decisions about worship themes, appropriate Scriptures, musical selections, and worship components. In most congregations it would be disastrous to have every member of the staff team that participates in worship independently design his or her own piece of the pie. A level of centralized decision making is required to ensure worship flow. Other types of ministries are often administered in a more decentralized fashion. Decisions about small groups and educational venues may be made by a variety of staff team members in different decision-making settings.

All staff teams demonstrate a tendency to settle into decision making somewhere along a continuum of choices, with high centralization on one end of the continuum and high decentralization on the other end. The style of decision-making (either centralized, decentralized, or somewhere in the middle) is often determined by the operating culture or theology of the congregation. However, the size of the congregation also has a great deal to do with how centralized or decentralized decision-making might be.

The small to mid-sized congregation is centralized by default. There just aren't that many people on the staff team to make decisions, so everything stays close to the senior clergy leader. In the professional size congregation, the staff team still operates as a fairly centralized decision-making body. However, one characteristic of the professional church is a constant unresolved pull toward decentralization. The head of staff is often stretched too thin to be engaged in all of the decision making, but the staff team is not large enough to establish effective smaller venues for decision making that don't involve the head of staff. Staff members (including the head of staff) wish that the head of staff could be less involved in day-to-day decision making, but the team isn't quite ready to take the leap into a more decentralized approach.

Decision making in the strategic church becomes much more decentralized by necessity. The staff team meets in too many different venues, and there are simply too many ministries and staff members for the head of staff to remain engaged in every decision. In this size congregation an executive team often emerges as a strategic body that assigns decision making to appropriate subsections of the staff team.

Finally, a congregation that is in the matrix size category works with a fully decentralized decision-making structure. Each segment of the staff team receives strong messages about the strategic direction of the congregation, but then growth is managed everywhere, all at the same time. It's not unusual in this size congregation for ministry areas to design and launch programs that the head of staff is not consulted about, but only hears about as the programs come to fruition. The head of staff typically retains veto power but rarely engages it. There is a great deal of clarity in this congregation about what level of authority any given member of the team has, but no member of the team has a central decision-making role. Typically an executive pastor and business administrator will work jointly as an executive leadership team, ensuring that the flow of decision making remains effective.

Span of Control

How many employees will report to a single manager or supervisor? The question is an important one. The supervisory relationship is where staff members learn what the expectations of the congregation are for their role. It is also where the employee receives ongoing feedback about how she is performing against expectations. It is the relationship through which a staff member communicates her ideas, hopes, and dreams back to the organization. If a supervisor has too many direct reports, he or she is unable to provide effective supervision.

We say that an organization has a wide span of control if supervisors have a large number of employees reporting to them. They have a narrower span of control if they have just a few direct reports. Here is a diagram of an organization with a narrow span of control. A narrow span of control produces an organizational chart that is tall and narrow. You can see in this example that no manager or supervisor has more than two direct reporting relationships to manage.

Figure 5.1 A Narrow Span of Control

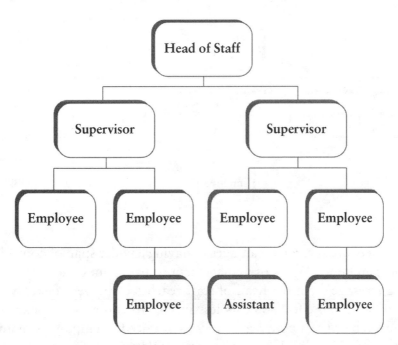

There are a number of advantages to a narrower span of control. Fewer reporting relationships allow a supervisor to communicate more easily and therefore more frequently with his employees, thus providing more effective individual supervision. The feedback of ideas from employees to their direct supervisor is easier, enabling good two-way communication.

The disadvantage of a narrow span of control is that the number of levels in the organization can multiply quickly. There is greater distance between the head of staff and the entry-level employees. This can create the feeling that there is a lot red tape to cut through to get things done in the congregation. The introduction of extra levels of management can also add to salary expense as the extra levels of supervision require higher levels of compensation. People have to be paid for the skill of supervision.

An example of an organization with a wide span of control is shown in the diagram below. You'll see that the organization is flatter, with fewer supervisors:

Figure 5.2 A Wide Span of Control

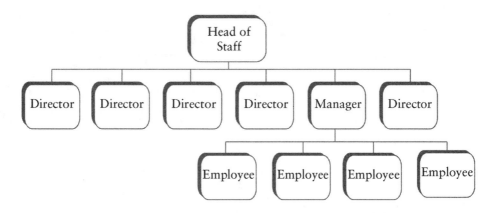

There are several advantages to having a wider span of control. There are fewer layers of management to pass a message through, so a message from the head of staff reaches employees faster and more accurately. It also costs less money to run a wider span of control, because a congregation does not need to employ as many managers. The disadvantage is that employees receive much less individual attention from their supervisors. Employees in this type of structure often report that they don't know what is expected of them and they don't receive regular feedback about how they are doing.

Inevitably, congregational leaders want to know what the "right number" of direct reports is for a head of staff in a large congregation. And the answer is . . . it depends. It depends upon how well employees know their roles, how similar the roles are, whether the employees work at the same location as the supervisor, and a host of other factors. Generally speaking, I tell leaders that their span of control is too wide (i.e., they have too many direct reports) if they find themselves unable to host individual supervisory meetings with each direct report at least biweekly.

Different size congregations have different span-of-control issues. Span of control is typically not much of an issue in the multi-celled congregation. The organizational structure is flat (i.e., everyone reports to the senior clergy person), and the small size of the staff team allows for a manageable span of control for the head of staff. The professional church experiences a great deal of tension around span-of-control issues. As the congregation professionalizes its ministry, a significant number of program managers are added, all of whom initially report to the head of staff. Eventually the strain the head of staff experiences in managing all of these relationships (or the lack of attention received by program areas) forces a re-organization into a taller structure with more layers of management and narrower spans of control. The effective strategic church is almost always organized in this way. Congregations of this size continue to grow the staff team by adding new departments, each with its own narrow span of control. Finally, the matrix congregation often maintains manageable spans of control by setting up dual reporting structures. (More will be said about this in the next section.)

CONGREGATIONAL SIZE AND STAFF TEAM DESIGN

Let's recall the organizational design questions explored in the previous section of this chapter.

1. What is the basis for dividing up the work? (Division of labor)
2. How will we integrate/coordinate the work? (Integrating Mechanisms)
3. Where will decision making be housed? (Centralization)
4. How many employees will report to a single manager/supervisor? (Span of Control)

We've examined each question individually, and we have explored how the answer to any one of these questions is likely to vary, given the size of the congregation asking the question. Now we put the answers to the four questions together to formulate an actual design for the staff team. It is not surprising that most staff designs in a particular size category will look similar, because of how the four questions were answered. We begin with the multi-celled congregation.

Figure 5.3 Typical Structure: The Multi-Celled Congregation

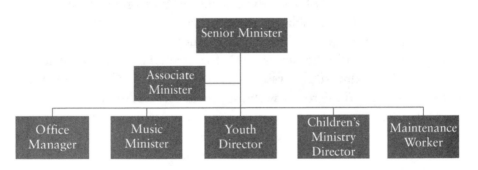

The staffing structure in the multi-celled congregation is rather simple. If the congregation has added an associate minister to the team, that associate functions very much as a generalist, serving the congregation in many ways as a backup to the senior minister. The associate may have one particular area of responsibility that has a specialist feel to it, such as education, discipleship, or small groups. More than likely, everyone on the staff team reports to the senior minister. The staff team is made up of an assortment of both generalist and specialist positions that function side by side. Most of the specialist positions (in this case the music minister, youth director, and children's ministry director) are part-time employees. The team coordinates its work primarily by being in one-on-one supervisory relationship with the senior minister, who functions as the overall coordinator. Any shared decision making takes place in a weekly staff meeting that incorporates every member of the team and perhaps some key volunteer roles.

Figure 5.4 Typical Structure: The Professional Church

The staffing structure most typically found in the professional church is a flat structure with a very wide span of control for the senior minister. This size congregation almost always has at least one full-time associate pastor and maybe two. The associates work alongside the senior minister to serve the worship, sacramental, and pastoral needs of the congregation, but each associate also has a specific area of specialization that occupies a good portion of his or her working hours. Everyone else on the staff team functions in a specialist role. The staff team meeting is used as the primary connecting mechanism through which members of the team integrate their work. As the congregation reaches the upper end of the attendance range in this category, the senior minister feels increasingly stressed. Staff members are finding that they don't get enough one-on-one supervision time. It becomes increasingly difficult to run effective staff meetings that don't simply turn into reporting venues.

Figure 5.5 Typical Structure: The Strategic Church

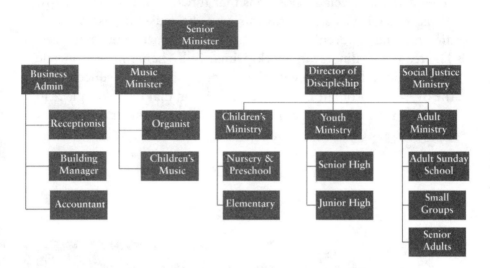

Everyone on the staff team in a strategic church is a full-blown specialist. The team as a whole is divided into identifiable departments with distinct ministry foci. Departments may be managed by ordained clergy specialists or program specialists who were hired for their expertise in particular ministry areas. When the collective staff team meets, it is for short periods of time and primarily for communication purposes. Each department has its own weekly or biweekly staff team meeting where important decision making and coordination of ministry occurs. The senior minister typically meets weekly with her direct reports to coordinate decision making at a more strategic level. This leadership level may be referred to as the executive team. Toward the upper end of this size range, congregations may introduce the role of executive pastor to oversee the programmatic side of the congregation.

Figure 5.6 Typical Structure: The Matrix Church

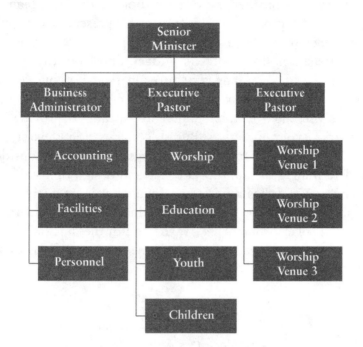

It is difficult to characterize the structure of the matrix congregation, because the structures vary widely. You'll see that the staff team at this size functions with a true executive team, made up of one or more executive pastors and the business administrator. In this particular design (which serves a multi-site congregation), one executive pastor oversees all of the campus pastors, while another executive pastor oversees all of the functional areas of ministry. Each functional ministry area (worship, education, youth and children) has a dual reporting relationship. The primary supervisor is the executive pastor, but each area also has dotted-line (or secondary) reporting relationships to each of the worship venue pastors. In this way they are each part of multiple and distinct ministry teams at all times. In this way, decision making has become fully decentralized, with staff in each location making choices about what best suits their venue.

Reading through a chapter like this one may leave the reader with the impression that the organization of the staff team is a rather scientific process. The information presented here might seem to suggest that you simply look up the attendance range of a congregation along with its budget, and from that you can determine the ideal staffing structure. In fact, nothing could be further from the truth. Organizational design is an art form. The guidelines presented in this chapter are meant to provide some benchmarks, typical practices. But no congregation is ever typical. The nuances of life in any given congregation must be considered when determining the appropriate size and design of a staff team. Your congregation has a missional focus that is uniquely formed by your community context, the giftedness of your leaders, and the passions of your members. At the end of the day, the size and design of your staff team must serve the missional focus of your congregation. No two staff designs are ever the same.

QUESTIONS FOR INDIVIDUAL OR GROUP REFLECTION

1. Who do you include in your definition of *staff* in your congregation? Does that designation include any volunteer positions? Which volunteer roles in your congregation might satisfy the term *staff* as it is used in this chapter?

2. What percentage of your annual operating budget is dedicated to payroll-related expenses? Consult the chart on page 118 of this text, where staff costs as a percentage of budget are portrayed for various attendance ranges. How does the percentage of your budget dollars allocated to payroll compare to the averages shown?

3. Which, if any, of the following circumstances might be influencing your payroll costs? (See page 119 for a description of how these factors might affect the amount you spend on payroll.)

a. Are you growing?

b. What is the dominant age group in your congregation?

c. How old is your congregation (What year were you founded?)

d. Where is your church located?

e. What is the predominant racial identity of your congregation?

f. What proportion of your staff is part-time?

g. What is the socioeconomic status of the community you serve?

4. What is your ratio of FTE (Full-time Equivalent) staff to average number of weekend attendees? How does this number compare to the averages listed on page 120? Does this number seem to indicate that you are overstaffed, understaffed, or appropriately staffed for your size?

5. Does your staff team design provide adequate administrative support? Calculate the number of FTE clergy staff, program staff, and administrative support staff you employ. Compare that number to the averages shown in the chart on page 122. What does this comparison suggest about your administrative support staffing levels?

6. This chapter discussed four basic design features that inform staff team design: division of labor, integrating mechanisms, centralization, and span of control. How would you describe the staff team design of your congregation in each of these four areas? Place an "X" on each continuum on the next page to reflect the leanings of your current staff team design.

Division of Labor

←——————————————————————————————→

Generalized Roles   Specialized Roles

Integrating Mechanisms

←——————————————————————————————→

Unified Staff Meeting   Decentralized Decision Makings

Centralization in Decision Making

←——————————————————————————————→

Centralized Decision Making   Specialized Roles

Span of Control

←——————————————————————————————→

Wide Span of Control   Narrow Span of Control

If you placed the majority of your Xs toward the left side of the chart, you most likely have a staff team design that is relatively flat, with few layers of middle management. If you placed the majority of your Xs toward the right side of the chart, your staff design is probably taller, with more intermediary decision-making and reporting structures. Which aspects of your design seem to be working for you and which are problematic, given the size of the congregation?

CHAPTER 6

Governance and Board Function

IN CONGREGATIONAL LIFE, THE TERM *GOVERNING* REFERS TO THE LEGITI-mate right of a leadership body (board, council, session, and so forth) to exercise authority over the congregation. *Governance* is how a board goes about exercising authority in the life of the congregation; it is the system or process for managing the decisions and affairs of congregational leadership.[1]

Congregational governance involves two significant leadership subsystems—the board and the staff team. Jointly these bodies must negotiate who takes initiative in managing and leading the congregation. Will the congregation be primarily led by its board or by its staff team? Or will it be collaboratively led by both, and if so, what does that arrangement look like? What distinguishes the work of the staff team from the work of the board, and how do the two entities manage to work together without stepping on one another's toes or becoming gridlocked? How do the head of staff and the board chairperson function as coleaders of the congregation?

Bridgewater Baptist Church has recently completed a strategic planning process. The planning was initiated by the pastor's council, an executive team of seven individuals, handpicked by the senior pastor from the church council, a 50-member leadership body. The planning involved a fairly comprehensive self-study. Although the study and the creation of the plan were facilitated by a small group of leaders, over 700 church members participated in surveys and listening sessions.

Initially, the church council and the congregation embraced the strategic plan. There was a great deal of excitement about moving in new directions, particularly around the strategic initiative of broadening lay leader involvement in the life of the church. However, three months after the adoption of the new strategic plan, trouble is beginning to brew. The staff team is trying to implement the plan, but thus far lay leaders aren't able to figure out what role, if any, they have in bringing the new plan to fruition.

Furthermore, church members are beginning to question the basic authority of the pastor's council. What control does the congregation have over who gets appointed to that council and how long people get to serve on it? Church council members are expressing displeasure over their perception that they are frequently asked to rubber-stamp decisions already made by this inside group of leaders. Attendance at council meetings has become abysmal, and the nominating committee is having trouble recruiting new council leaders. The word is out that the council doesn't do very interesting work and that serving on the council is a frustrating waste of time.

Church members are beginning to wonder whether the way in which the church conducts its business is even Baptist. The church operates with a congregational form of polity, and every voice is supposed to be represented in the decision making of the church. The present system doesn't seem to honor the voice of the lay leaders who were elected to represent the congregation, let alone the average voice in the pew.

The story is not a new one. Confusion around leadership authority has always been a theme within faith communities. Who gets to lead? Which voices count in decision making? Who decides where authority resides? In Numbers 12, we encounter a remarkably familiar set of issues. The Israelite community has left the safety of Mount Sinai and is again traveling through the wilderness. Seventy elders have been appointed to assist Moses, and the leadership of the community seems certain and strong. Then there is a plague, and chaos breaks loose. The worst of the turmoil is instigated by two inside leaders, Aaron and Miriam, who begin questioning why Moses gets to be in charge. Why should their brother get to speak on behalf of God? Hadn't God also worked and spoken through Miriam and Aaron?

It is a leadership squabble of enough significance that God sees fit to intervene. The Lord descends in a pillar of cloud, and both Miriam and Aaron are struck with leprosy. Case closed. It's apparent whom God has designated to speak with authority. Unfortunately, faith communities today don't often receive such clear and strong signals from God about how authority structures ought to work. We are left to struggle with questions about the balance of authority, responsibility, and accountability in our decision-making structures.

GOVERNANCE AND SIZE

As a congregation enters the professional size category, a key organizational focus is the growth and professionalization of the staff team. As the staff team becomes more specialized and increasingly takes over the management function of the church, the governing body of the church is often thrown into a tailspin. If the staff team is going to run the church, what are the roles of laity, volunteers, and ultimately the board? Often, boards misunderstand their oversight charge and fail to relinquish management responsibilities of the church to the staff team. They end up micromanaging the senior clergy leader and staff. In these congregations the staff team and board become antagonistic toward one another. How is the staff team supposed to manage the church if the board won't relinquish some level of control?

The fundamental tension that is often at work in the governance of the large church is the push/pull between the complementary systems of strategic management and strategic leadership. Most governing bodies are clear that they should not be involved, and do not want to be involved, in the mundane operational tasks of the church—things like the design of worship, the selection of curriculum for education classes, the format of youth ministry small groups, and the like. However, boards are often not clear about whether they want to spend their time on leadership or management, and what distinguishes the two.

Consider this example. A congregation is working to create an environment that is more hospitable to visitors. This is one of the strategic initiatives named by the congregation. In support of this initiative, the hospitality committee and the staff team leader who oversees Sunday morning hospitality want to eliminate the current hospitality team of ushers and replace it with a more comprehensive cadre of greeters and hospitality captains. The change is meant to introduce a new congregational culture around hospitality, helping people see that hospitality is everyone's job. The change is going to be met with much interest by the congregation, both in support of and in opposition to eliminating the longstanding usher team. What is the board's involvement in this decision? Must board members approve it, be consulted about it, or be informed about it? Do they even need to know? Do they have veto power to stop it if they don't think that it is a move in the right direction? And if the board does involve itself in this decision, what part of the decision should they tackle? If we were to sit in on the board meeting and the staff meeting where the change was introduced, would the conversations sound similar or different?

In the broadest sense, leadership is about influencing an organization toward a common goal. Management is about orchestrating the actions of the organization, either to maintain a status quo or to produce a targeted change. Both boards and staff teams regularly engage in acts of both leadership and management. However, *strategic leadership* and *strategic management* are more nuanced versions of the broader terms and help to clarify the distinctions between the work of the board and the work of the staff team.

Strategic leadership involves discerning and articulating the mission and vision of the congregation; claiming core values; anticipating opportunities and threats that may impact the congregation's future; naming the strategic priorities of the congregation; and setting up accountability systems to ensure that the strategic priorities are tended to. *Strategic management* involves the creation of systems, processes, and programs that bring the missional priorities of the congregation to fruition, along with monitoring and evaluating those systems. In the broadest sense, in the large church the board takes responsibility for the strategic leadership of the congregation, and the staff team takes responsibility for strategic management. In practice, the distinction is never a simple one, and there are many grey areas about who is in charge of what.

As boards struggle to find their place in the strategic leadership and strategic management of their congregations, they tend to move back and forth along three continuums.[2]

More Involvement vs. Less Involvement

Every governing body struggles with how much board members need to know about the day-to-day life of the congregation, what decisions they need to make, what decisions they have a right to reverse, and when they need to be informed about decisions that others have made. Board members who support the more-involvement end of the continuum assert that is it important to know what is going on in the congregation. Board members must actively participate in the ministry of the congregation as key volunteers, financial supporters, and overseers. At the more-involvement end of the continuum, leaders remind themselves that while the ministry belongs to the congregation, the board members are the trustees of the ministry. It is the responsibility of board members to remain hyper-vigilant on behalf of the congregation.

At some point, the board that is highly involved in the work of the staff team and the life of the congregation begins to experience some of the downsides associated with deep involvement. In board meetings leaders have a hard time staying focused on the larger picture of the congregation's direction. Staff members report feeling disempowered, never thinking they can make decisions without first checking in with the board. And so the board does some self-correction and moves toward the less-involvement end of the continuum. Initially the move feels good. Leaders regain some of their bigger-picture perspective. Board meetings become shorter, sharper, and more focused. Staff members feel energized by the sudden ability to act without censure and oversight. Until something critical happens in the operational life of the congregation that the board isn't aware of. Then a self-correction takes place once again, back to the more-involved end of the continuum.

Over-control vs. Under-control

Boards that can't quite figure out why they exist often adopt some form of micromanagement to fill the void. Board members know that the role is supposed to be important, but they can't find worthy work to do every month. They become watchdogs over the staff team, heavily involved in administration and serving on committees that allow them to keep a close eye on staff team activity. Tight control is seen as the road to staff accountability. When taken to its logical extreme, living on this end of the continuum produces adversarial relationships between board and staff members.

In reaction to declining staff-board relationships, boards will often self-correct by moving towards the under-control end of the spectrum. Under-controlling boards often become cheerleaders for the staff team. The hallmark of this board is blind trust and support. They may refrain from asking any hard questions because to do so would demonstrate a lack of faith in their hired leaders. Rubber-stamping the requests of staff and committee leaders is a common practice on this side of the continuum.

Past vs. Present vs. Future Focus

Some boards spend a good deal of their time examining the work the staff team has already done. The regular meeting of this board is spent receiving reports on what has been accomplished to date. Conversation of the board is focused on reviewing, rehashing, and redoing the staff and committee work of the church. In keeping with the focus on the past, this board will consistently find itself in reactive mode, responding to the initiative of the staff team, rather than acting proactively to guide the congregation.

Other boards invest themselves too fully in the present-day decision making of the church. Staff members bring their present dilemmas to the board meeting, and board members help the staff figure out what to do next in the execution of their ministry.

At the opposite end of this spectrum is the board that remains so future-focused that it loses track of where the congregation is right now. Some boards become so fully invested in long-term thinking, dreaming, and planning that they forget to evaluate what is happening in the present and to determine how the present is positioning the congregation to live into its future.

MODES OF GOVERNANCE

In the book *Governance as Leadership,* authors Richard Chait, William Ryan, and Barbara Taylor posit that there are three modes of governance that boards must simultaneously satisfy, and when all three of these modes are tended, the board is doing effective governance work.[3] The paragraphs that follow apply these definitions of governance to life in the large congregation.

Governance as Fiduciary Work

A board that is working in fiduciary mode is tending to the stewardship of tangible assets, the fundamental work of trusteeship. This governance mode ensures that the congregation is being faithful to its mission, accountable for its performance, and compliant with relevant laws and legislation.[4]

The fiduciary mode of governance is aimed at preventing theft, waste, and the misuse of resources. In this mode the board spends its time ensuring that resources are deployed effectively and efficiently in service to the congregation's mission. The board is safeguarding the mission of the congregation against both unintentional drift and unauthorized shifts in purpose. This work typically involves the oversight of audits, budgets, investments, compensation, facilities, fundraising, and the performance of the senior clergy leader, as well as the enactment of policies and practices that discourage waste, prevent abuse, and promote efficiency.

The boards of most congregations spend the vast majority of their time working in the fiduciary mode of governance. The fact that most boards spend their time here becomes the primary determinant of the type of person recruited to serve on the board. But members are people who enjoy engaging in the fiduciary work of the congregation, such as accountants, bankers, real estate managers, insurance reps, and the like.

Governance as Strategic Work

In strategic mode the board is working to set the congregation's priorities and is seeing that time, talent, financial, and capital resources are being deployed in accordance with those missional priorities. When tending to this mode of governance, the board's focus shifts from conformance to performance. Leaders are seeking to match internal strengths and weaknesses against external opportunities and threats in pursuit of the congregation's mission. The strategic work of the board is much broader than overseeing a process of strategic planning. It clearly involves things like writing mission and vision statements, naming core values, and creating plans to accomplish strategic priorities, but it goes beyond these traditional elements of strategic planning. This mode of governance is also about influencing the congregation to act in strategic ways by strengthening congregational identity, examining outmoded assumptions, and creating strategic responses to environmental change.[5]

Often the real challenge for a board trying to govern more strategically grows out of the fact that the board spends so much of its time in fiduciary mode that board members are typically recruited for their fiduciary orientation. Strategic work requires different skills and a different mindset from fiduciary work. Leaders who are good at fiduciary management may not be drawn toward strategic thinking, and vice versa. Meetings that are crafted to tend to the fiduciary work of the board don't serve strategic governance well. Boards that do good strategic work often function with more flexible board structures, more adaptable agendas, and smaller board and committee structures than boards that primarily work in fiduciary mode.

Governance as Generative Work

As congregations face internal threats and external opportunities, they are often required to engage in fundamental changes in their approach to ministry. Generative thinking is what occurs somewhere between the insights of individuals that something is changing and the paradigm shift that the congregation as a whole makes in response to that change. When leaders are working generatively, others often express admiration for their wisdom and insight. Generative work includes things like paying attention to clues and cues, choosing and using frames to understand challenges, and constructing narrative themes that make meaning out of an experience. This is work that all governing boards should be engaging regularly.[6]

The challenge of generative work at the board level is that there isn't an easy organizational construct to hold it. Fiduciary mode emerges naturally and easily as a body of work for a board to do. Typical board and meeting structures encourage the kind of representational reporting that so often moves boards into a fiduciary mindset. Strategic work is a little more difficult to enter into, but a board retreat or the work of a strategic planning subcommittee can invite a board into more strategic mindset.

Generative work is open and free flowing. It requires unencumbered space to develop. As such, it is the least well represented governance mode on most congregational boards. The generative work of the congregation is more likely to originate with the senior clergy leader, on the staff team, or in the committees of the congregation. This puts the governing board in a reactive stance instead of a proactive one. If we want our boards to do more effective governance, we need to create space and venues for generative thinking to occur at the board level.

Congregational Size and Governance Mode

Boards in every size congregation must tend to all three modes of governance—fiduciary, strategic, and generative. In the large congregation a board must come to terms with the fact that many of the fiduciary responsibilities of the board can be delegated. The board can never abdicate its responsibility for fiduciary oversight, but it can rely on board committees and the staff team to do much of the fiduciary work on its behalf.

The board of the multi-celled congregation tends to live predominantly in fiduciary mode. The staff team in this size congregation is not yet large enough to assume the full managerial responsibilities of the church, and lay leaders are still actively involved in the management of ministry. This situation tends to result in board meetings that are very focused on day-to-day managerial issues. The board of the multi-celled congregation knows that it is supposed to be spending time on the strategic direction of the church but can never quite figure out how to get there. Board members fear that relinquishing their focus on the more fiduciary aspects of governance will results in an organizationally ineffective congregation.

The governing board in the professional size congregation is intuitively drawn toward a more balanced focus between the fiduciary and strategic modes. The largest struggle of the board in this size congregation is figuring out how to work more frequently in strategic mode and how to inject some element of generative thinking into its ongoing work. The size of the professional staff team in this size congregation is expanding, and leaders struggle with how to represent the voice of the staff team on the board. When all of the professional clergy sit on the board, meetings often turn into reporting venues for staff members to strut their stuff. Board members increasingly wonder what the role of lay leaders is in running a congregation that has become so staff driven.

Most congregations in the strategic and matrix size categories have learned some things about delegating the managerial work of the board, so that more time can be spent in strategic and generative mode. The governing body in this congregation has typically been downsized to create a more nimble decision-making body. The staff team is represented by the senior clergy leader and the executive pastor. Other professional staff members attend board meetings only when invited, to evaluate or reflect upon a particular aspect of ministry that rests within the staff member's sphere of influence. This practice sometimes results in staff members feeling disconnected from the strategic thinking of leadership.

Governing boards in the strategic and matrix congregation know they need to invest themselves more fully in the strategic mode, but they often struggle with shaping good conversations around strategy. For example, a board ends up spending the better part of four meetings talking about whether to move the bell from the old building to the new building. They know that there is a strategic issue somewhere at work in the dilemma about the bell, but they can't quite figure out how to have a meaningful conversation about it without reverting back into fiduciary mode.

A MODEL OF GOVERNANCE

Board structures in the large congregation are always in a state of flux, moving along the three continuums described earlier and moving among the three modes of governance. The continual struggle to stay focused on worthy work that honors the tensions around involvement, control, and present vs. future orientation leaves many board members feeling whiplash. What is the right way to think about the work of the board compared to the work of the staff team?

Alban senior consultant Dan Hotchkiss has crafted a model of board leadership that I believe is particularly well suited to the large congregation. He explores the model and identifies a way to transition into the model in his book *Governance and Ministry: Rethinking Board Leadership*.[7] In the section that follows I will provide a brief overview of the Hotchkiss model. I refer the reader to the original text for a more in-depth treatment of the topic.

The Hotchkiss model begins with the premise that an effective congregation requires the following:

- A unified structure for making *governance* decisions. The governing board represents the members by articulating mission and vision, evaluating programs, and ensuring responsible stewardship of resources.
- A unified structure for making *ministry* decisions. Staff leaders work harmoniously to create effective programs, with the support of a performance management system that sets expectations and provides feedback.
- A firm and well-marked boundary, with active communication and accountability between governance and ministry.[8]

Governance and Ministry

In this model the words *governance* and *ministry* differentiate between two spheres of leadership in the congregation. *Governance* includes the tasks of articulating the mission, selecting a strategy for getting there, making sure it happens, and ensuring that people and property are protected against harm. *Ministry* is most of the rest of what a congregation does—achieving the internal and external results the congregation exists to serve. Anyone whose job it is to lead a program, teach a class, serve food, lead worship, or help a visitor to find a seat is part of ministry. So are people who provide indirect support by training others, writing checks, sweeping floors, and tuning the piano. Ministry, to put it simply, is the "doing" aspect of the congregation.[9]

The difference between governance and ministry is not hard versus soft, money versus faith, strategic versus tactical, top versus bottom, or business versus people. Both governance and ministry concern themselves with faith and values, both involve prayer and discernment, both require strategic thinking, and both require decisions about how to employ the financial, capital, and human resources of the congregation.

A simple way to distinguish between governance and ministry is to look at the outcomes produced by each. Both governance and ministry, when effectively executed, produce positive relationships, enthusiasm, and renewed faith. Governance produces minutes, policies, mission statements, goals, and strategic-planning documents. Ministry brings into being worship services, study groups, mission trips, service projects, well-maintained buildings, thriving families, and renewed hope.[10]

The relationship between the two is illustrated in figure 6.1 on the following page and further explained in the paragraphs that follow.[11]

Figure 6.1 shows governance and ministry as two overlapping curves that together define three zones—at the left, governance; at the right, ministry; and in the middle, a zone of overlap for the strategy and discernment work shared by the two. At the top of

Figure 6.1 The Hotchkiss Governance-Ministry Model

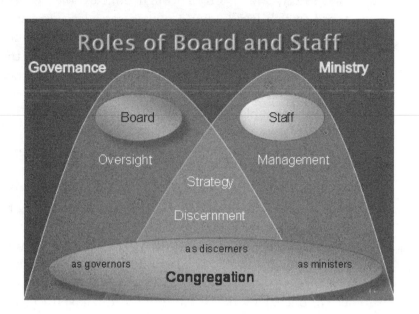

each curve is its most frequent decision maker, typically the board for governance and the staff for ministry.

In the Hotchkiss model, governance and ministry do not function in isolation from each other. They connect in several clearly defined ways:

- First, there is a zone of overlap at the bottom center of the diagram for issues that need input from both governance and ministry before traveling upward to the right or left for a decision. The distinction becomes sharper at the point of decision—at the top of each curve. Below these summits, the atmosphere is more collaborative. Clear decision-making authority at the top actually makes it easier to share information, power, and influence throughout the organization.
- Second, the governing board connects with ministry leaders by adopting policies to guide their work. These policies include mission and vision statements annual goals

and budgets and rules about finance, personnel, real estate, personal safety, and so on. Through policies, the governing board (which legally could make every decision itself) delegates authority to ministry leaders and gives them guidance about how that authority should be used. In effect, the board sets a limit to its own agenda—deciding in advance that it will focus on its governance role, instead of trying to duplicate or supplant the work of ministry leaders in the daily management of congregational life.

- Third, the governing board holds the staff accountable. Responsible boards match delegated power with accountability—neither writing a blank check to ministry leaders nor holding them responsible for a result without first giving them adequate authority to accomplish it. Having delegated power responsibly, the board monitors the work through regular reports and sees that individual performance is evaluated regularly. Accountability begins at home: No one step a board can take instills a spirit of accountability throughout the congregation more effectively than instituting regular evaluation of its own performance.[12]

The congregation is depicted at the bottom of the diagram, not because it is less powerful than the board or the staff team, but because it is foundational and members serve in all three zones. As the diagram suggests, the distinction between governance and ministry is more important to leaders than to members. Most members do not need to think at all about the difference between governance and ministry. Members serve regularly as doers, discerners, and decision makers in ministry, without consciously needing to make the distinction.

The Roles of Committees and Teams

The boundary between governance and ministry in the Hotchkiss model leads to a stricter definition of board committees. True board committees, by definition, exist to help the board do the board's work. Every board functions with a few permanent committees. Those committees are determined by the unique needs of each congregation. A typical congregation may function with a governance committee (to recruit and train new board members), a finance committee (to assist the board in its fiduciary responsibilities around finance and budgeting), and a personnel or human resources (HR) committee (to assist the board in overseeing the performance management function of the congregation.) On occasion, the board will need to form additional task forces for delegated work, but all task forces should be temporary and dissolved upon completion of their task. This prevents the excessive proliferation of committees in the large congregation.

The small groups of leaders who gather regularly to plan and execute the ministry functions of the congregation are not board committees. Hotchkiss uses the term *ministry teams* to refer to the groups that plan and carry out worship, pastoral care, mission, service, education, discipleship, building maintenance, membership, and so forth. Ministry teams are different from board committees in several remarkable ways. They are not representative in nature. Group members are not chosen for their interest or ability in establishing policy or their representation of a viewpoint. They are chosen for their passion and knowledge in a specific ministry area, making them oriented toward action and problem-solving, with a strong preference for action over talk. Ministry teams do not report to the governance side of leadership; they report to the ministry side of leadership. This means that the staff team takes responsibility for coordinating and overseeing the work of ministry teams. Placing teams on the ministry side of the diagram is an important part of the strategy for keeping the board focused on the work of governance and not getting sidetracked into conversations about day-to-day ministry.

Governing by Policy

"Governing by policy" is the means by which a board oversees the ministry of the congregation, without stepping into management mode. To focus its attention, a board has to put firm boundaries around its own agenda. It remains responsible for everything under its authority, but controls some things directly, shares control of others, and fully delegates yet others. The primary tool that a board uses to set up healthy delegation is the policy statement. A policy is an authoritative written statement designed to control many individual decisions over time. Hotchkiss proposes that every governing board establish four broad categories of policy in order to facilitate effective delegation.[13]

- **Discernment:** This segment of policy addresses the congregation's mission. Typical products of this work include mission and vision statements, core values, and strengths to preserve.
- **Strategy:** The strategic plan contains the longer-range plans of the congregation (one to five years out). A strategic plan outlines the major choices that have been made about how the congregation will seek to fulfill its mission, including strategic priorities, annual goals and objectives, and corresponding action plans.
- **Management:** Policies on management serve to delegate part of the board's power and authority to others. Within these policies the board clearly articulates the results that it wants, the extent and limits of the power and authority it is prepared to delegate, and a plan for evaluation and accountability. A board will need to create policies related to the care of people (health and safety, nondiscrimination, and the like), staff (compensation and benefits, grievance processes, and so forth) and resources (insurance, document retention, and so on).
- **Oversight:** This set of policies sets standards for the congregation's life and work by establishing a plan for monitoring and evaluating that work, so staff and volunteer program leaders are accountable, and the congregation learns from its experience. These policies may incorporate topics such as financial reporting, staff reports, financial audits, annual performance evaluation of staff, program evaluation, and so forth.

How It All Works Together

What if your governing body has decided that it needs to make more space for strategic and generative work, and therefore is seeking to more effectively delegate ministry leadership to the staff team? Large congregations moving in this direction tend to surface a predictable set of questions around the transition. As previously mentioned, Hotchkiss's *Governance and Ministry* is a solid resource for congregations in the midst of this transition. He covers the creation of a policy handbook and a model for transition. I will not try to reproduce that discussion here. Instead, I will step outside the Hotchkiss model and focus on those questions that seem particularly relevant in a large church context.

Board Size and Representation

The reader will remember from chapter 2 that I talked about the basic organizational building blocks that make up congregational structures. I differentiated between decision-making groups, care-and-support groups, family groups, and community groups—four distinct organizational bodies in the life of a congregation. Boards and their committees clearly fall into the decision-making group category. The fiduciary, strategic, and generative work of boards and committees fundamentally involves making decisions on behalf of the congregation. This is work that is best done in groups of five to seven individuals. Groups that grow larger than this have passed the upper limit for group effectiveness in decision making. Many members of large congregations think that they couldn't possibly operate with a board of this size, because such a small group couldn't represent the full diversity of membership. Let's look at the repercussions of that thinking.

When representation is the key feature that informs board recruitment, three things happen that ultimately lead to bad governance. First, the board grows larger and larger as leaders feverishly try to ensure representation of all groups in the congregation.

Ultimately, the representation strategy fails. It becomes virtually impossible to create a governing body that mirrors the full complexity of the large congregation. Special-interest groups within the congregation begin critiquing board makeup, and some individuals are always dissatisfied with their lack of voice on the board. The board grows so large that it loses the ability to effectively solve problems. The board begins doing the only kind of work that a group of its size can do, reporting on activity that has already taken place and engaging in community care. Effective governance goes by the wayside.

Second, when board members are recruited because they represent specific demographics, they tend to protect constituencies over mission. Knowing that they were selected for the board because of their gender, age, social group, or ministry passions, they feel compelled to protect the special interests of the groups that they perceive they have been selected to represent. Rather than making decisions that will promote the mission of the congregation, board members promote the special interests of their people, however they self-define "their" people—the choir, the senior adults, the young adults, or the women of the congregation. The average board meeting becomes an exercise in balancing the cares and concerns of competing interest groups, rather than an exercise in promoting the mission of the congregation.

Finally, when board members are recruited with a focus on representation, they are recruited for the wrong skills. If people are selected to represent a demographic or ministry area, it is likely that they are oriented toward action in that ministry. Effective board leaders are skilled strategic and generative thinkers, people who will invest themselves in the formation of policy and are invested in building systems of accountability. Selecting a musical person to serve on the governing board, because she can represent the best interest of the choirs, is likely to frustrate both the board and the individual. If the music member doesn't possess the skill set needed to govern well, she shouldn't serve on the board, regardless of the demographic she represents.

Board members in the large church should be recruited primarily for demonstrated or potential skills in governance leadership.

All board members should understand that they represent the full congregational body in their decision making. As much as possible, board members need to step beyond the biases of their particular interest groups to act on behalf of the larger mission.

Having said this, it is always important that a board be perceived as having the ability to act on behalf of the full congregation. Some attention to board diversity is a must. If people don't see enough diversity on the board, they will not feel represented by the board, regardless of the leadership skills present. An all white, male, middle-aged board will be suspect in a congregation that values diversity. People need to be able to look at their governing leaders and recognize themselves in the mix.

The Role of an Executive Committee

Some congregations simply cannot imagine reducing the size of their governing boards to five to seven individuals. Either the operating culture or the congregation's polity system does not support a streamlined decision-making group. Congregation members may be too distrustful of the small board, believing that it couldn't possibly represent the best interests of an entire congregation. In these congregations an executive committee (EC) can be formed within the board structure to facilitate more effective decision making and to help the board maintain a focus that is more strategic and generative.

In large boards, executive committees typically consist of the senior clergy leader, the executive clergy (if such a role exists), the board chair, the treasurer (or other financial officer), and one or two other central board figures. Executive committees may meet weekly, biweekly, or monthly, depending upon the work that they do on behalf of the congregation. Executive committees can promote good governance when they focus their time in the following ways:

Triage: One of the primary ways an executive committee can promote good governance is by triaging the various topics that are slated to come before a board. The team looks over all of the slated board issues and determines which topics can be effectively delegated to other decision-making bodies in the congregation. By keeping an overabundance of managerial items off the agenda, the executive team can help the board spend more time on strategic and generative work.

Framing: Once the EC has determined that an issue belongs on the board's agenda, members can frame the issue in a way that will encourage strategic and generative conversations about the topic. They can determine which part, if any, of the "shall we move the bell?" conversation belongs to the board, and then they can frame the topic in such a way that the board's time is well used. For example, the EC may decide that the issue before the board is this, "Does the presence of the bell as a symbol of our identity and heritage warrant the cost involved in relocating the bell?" as opposed to "Should the bell be moved?"

Similarly, the EC may entertain some dialogue around important topics before bringing the issues to the board, so only those elements of the topic that are relevant to the board's decision making are brought to the board. In other words, the EC strains out irrelevant or misleading data, so the board conversation stays more focused on the truly critical issues at hand. The board does not need to know that Charlie's cousin's uncle has a crane that could be used to move the bell and that he is willing to lend the crane along with an operator to the church. The board simply needs to know what the final cost is likely to be, so it can make its strategic decision about its relocation.

Decision Making: Some boards delegate specific types of decision making to the EC. In other words the EC functions as a "real" governing board between meetings of the larger board, subject to approval of the full board. The decisions most commonly handled by an executive team are the time-sensitive issues that must be acted upon in between regularly scheduled board meetings. When the EC makes a decision on behalf of the board, it is critical that full disclosure of that decision be communicated back to board members in a timely manner.

Forming a "consent" agenda: A consent agenda, sometimes called a consent "calendar," is a component of a meeting agenda that enables the board to group routine items and resolutions under one umbrella. When a consent agenda is used, the board reaches a general agreement ahead of time on the use of the procedures. Issues that are packaged together in a consent agenda are distributed to board members ahead of the regularly scheduled meeting for preview purposes. At the meeting, items in the consent agenda do not warrant any discussion before a vote. Unless a board member thinks that an item should be discussed and requests the removal of that item ahead of time, the entire package is voted on at once without any additional explanations or comments. Because no questions or comments on these items are allowed during the meeting, this procedure saves time. Those items removed from the consent agenda by a member of the board can be discussed more fully before being acted upon.[14] The executive committee can sort the issues facing the board before the board meeting to determine which items can effectively be included within the consent agenda.

Large congregations that make effective use of an executive committee often find that over time, the board needs to meet less frequently. As the EC learns to more effectively triage, frame, and make decisions on behalf of the board, board members come to accept and expect strong leadership from the EC. Board members appreciate the need to meet less frequently and the fact that when they do meet, they are engaged in more productive conversations that truly benefit the life of the congregation. Some congregations, after working effectively with an executive committee over time, come to realize that the EC has become the governing board and that the larger governing body is actually an advisory group to the EC. Once this awareness takes hold, the congregation may be ready to reduce the size of its board to five to seven individuals and eliminate the need for an executive committee.

Board Involvement in the Budget

In all congregations the governing board bears ultimate responsibility for presenting the congregation with an annual budget that supports the mission of the congregation and keeps the congregation focused on its agreed-upon priorities. It is one of the fiduciary responsibilities of the governing board to submit an operating budget for congregational approval each year.

In the large congregation leaders often struggle to balance the input of both board and staff throughout the budgeting cycle. Governing bodies that overly invest in the managerial work of the congregation may believe that they need to hold tightly to the budgeting process from beginning to end. However, once a congregation has passed into the professional size category, the budgeting cycle will be most effective if it is initiated and managed by the staff team, not the board.

Early in the budgeting cycle, the board should provide the staff team with a statement of its priorities for the coming budget cycle. The board may suggest that it expects a certain cost-of-living increase for all of its staff members. The board may also indicate that it expects the new initiative concerning the addition of a worship service to be appropriately funded. Board members may indicate that the upgrade of IT equipment is important to them but not as critical as staff raises and launching the new worship service. With these broad strategic priorities in mind, staff leaders are empowered to shape the budget, bringing it back to the board for approval before presentation to the congregation.

Strategic Planning

It is clearly the board's responsibility to initiate and approve a strategic plan for the congregation (consisting of a mission statement, core values, strengths to preserve, strategic priorities, and action plans). But who actually does the work of planning—the study, the discernment, the articulation of priorities, and the creation of action plans? If the board is small enough and nimble enough, and if the board has effectively delegated much of its managerial work, board members may find that they are able to fully engage in the work of strategic planning on behalf of the congregation. Monthly board meetings focus on strategic, generative, and evaluative conversations. An annual retreat, including board and staff members, is used to establish the current year's priorities. If specific congregational studies need to be employed (congregational surveys, demographic studies, and listening sessions), the board may create a temporary ad hoc committee to do that work on its behalf.

When the board is not yet working in a manner that allows it to strategically plan on behalf of the congregation (because the board is too large or is still heavily engaged in managerial work), then the board may want to delegate the creation of the strategic plan to a smaller planning team. This team should still be temporary, accountable to the board, and dissolved once the plan has been developed and adopted. The strategic planning task force can facilitate the data gathering, schedule discernment venues where staff and board members come together to make meaning out of the data, and synthesize the learning into a strategic planning document. A study of this depth does not need to be repeated every year. The effective board will continually update its strategic plan, so over time, it becomes the strategic planning group and doesn't need an ongoing separate study team.

For more on how the strategic planning cycle is managed within the life of the large congregation, please see chapter 8, "Forming and Executing Strategy."

Providing Staff Oversight

Perhaps the most confusing piece of governance work that the board of the large church faces is how to provide oversight to, and require accountability of, the staff team. The board ends up delegating much of its managerial responsibility to the staff team over time. In the large church the staff team is overseeing ministry teams, running the building, administering finance, preparing budgets, and coordinating congregational care. Eventually, board members may think they don't know enough about what the staff team is doing to provide effective oversight. Some boards end up not paying any attention to the work of the staff team, believing that they don't have a meaningful role to play. Other boards know they are supposed to be providing oversight but may not have been able to figure out how. They often resort to micromanaging the team. They pick one or two areas of staff team life that they are determined to have some control over, and then they hound the staff with meaningless requests for information or overzealous suggestions about how the work ought to be accomplished.

There is a middle way. The effective board in the large congregation knows that its role is to ensure that a system of performance management is in place for the staff team. Every staff member has clarity about three sets of expectations:

- Essential functions of the job: The essential functions of a position are the central tasks that must be completed by the staff member in the day-to-day execution of her job. Essential functions are the duties inherent to the position. They describe what the staff member is expected to do to fulfill basic role expectations.
- Core competencies of the role: Core competencies describe the expectations about the basic character attributes, behaviors, and abilities of the person who is doing the job. Competencies describe *how* your staff members should conduct themselves as they execute their day-to-day responsibilities.
- Annual performance goals: These goals focus employees on the priorities of the organization. They provide the staff with direction about how to channel their energy, encouraging each employee to grow her area of work in specific ways over the next six- to twelve-month period. Goals change from year to year to reflect the evolving strategic priorities of the organization.[15]

Furthermore, a performance management system ensures that every member of the staff team has a supervisor who provides regular and ongoing feedback about how well the employee is meeting expectations in each of these three areas. A good performance management system also ensures that every employee receives an annual performance evaluation during which she receives feedback on the three areas of performance, and during which she sets goals with her supervisor for the coming performance cycle.

Let's examine the overall role of the governing board, the head of staff and the personnel committee in a good performance management system. The governing board establishes the personnel policies of the congregation and charges the senior clergy leader, as head of staff, with managing the team within the constraints of those policies. The governing board acts as the supervisor to the senior clergy leader. The board establishes the essential functions and core competencies of the senior clergy role. The board also sets the annual goals and objectives against which the senior clergy leader will be evaluated.

Every other member of the staff team reports to a direct supervisor who ultimately reports to the senior clergy leader. No one other than the senior clergy leader should report directly to the board. Each supervisor is responsible for establishing the essential functions, core competencies, and annual performance goals for their direct reports, subject to the approval of the senior clergy leader. Each supervisor is responsible for preparing and facilitating the annual performance review for every employee that reports to her.

The personnel committee is a committee of the governing board. This committee exists to help the governing board establish personnel policy and to help the board satisfy itself that the church is in compliance with its personnel policies. It is *not* the role of the personnel committee to supervise or evaluate staff, or to randomly receive complaints about staff from the congregation.

Many personnel committees get themselves in trouble by overinvesting in the governance responsibilities of the board or the managerial responsibilities of the head of staff. The specific level of involvement required to ensure policy compliance will vary depending upon the size of the congregation. When the staff team is large enough to include a human resources (HR) director, the personnel committee limits its oversight role to a cursory review of job descriptions, performance evaluation forms, and salary recommendations, in a manner that ensures compliance with stated policies and outcomes.

In smaller congregations the personnel committee may be invited, by the senior clergy, to more actively assist in the performance management process by: helping to write job descriptions, designing the performance appraisal form, conducting research on fair and equitable pay practices, advising on difficult personnel matters, and sitting in on disciplinary conversations with employees. It's critical to bear in mind that a committee that has been invited to engage in these HR activities does so at the discretion and invitation of the senior pastor or head of staff. The committee should never presume to initiate these activities of its own accord, as doing so would undermine the senior pastor's authority as head of staff.

In some traditions the personnel committee may also be asked to participate in the annual performance review of the senior pastor. However, it's important for the governing board to maintain overall responsibility for the performance evaluation of the head of staff and the alignment of the head of staff's goals with congregational goals. The personnel committee may help to gather and synthesize data to complete the review but should never take on overall responsibility for the evaluation itself.

Personnel committees that imagine they exist to advocate for the best interests of the staff or protect the best interests of the congregation often find themselves embroiled in hotbeds of triangulation (gossip). Personnel committees should make themselves available only in order to receive reports of potential employment policy violations. Any complaints about staff team performance need to be lodged directly with the employee in question or her direct supervisor. People who want to complain about the leadership of the senior pastor should be redirected back to the senior pastor to express any complaint. The only exception to this rule is a complaint that involves an issue of possible professional misconduct.

Personnel committees should avoid the practice of meeting one-on-one with employees just to check in and see how things are going. These practices tend to undermine supervisory relationships on the staff team by inviting employees to vent their displeasure with their supervisors. Most of the input received in such meetings is not appropriate fodder for the personnel committee but must be resolved through the supervisory relationship.[16]

The Church Board's Relationship with Other Boards

A characteristic of the large church is that the governing body of the congregation must often interact with one or more other boards. The congregation may operate a school that maintains its own board. The foundation of the church is likely to have its own board. The congregation may sponsor multiple 501(c)(3) organizations (e.g., a food pantry, homeless program, arts program, and so forth), and each of these organizations may function with its own governing body.

Often the congregation will try to maintain some sense of "ownership" control over these independent ministries by requiring a specific number of church members to serve on the board of the nonprofit. Some congregations try to connect boards by having a member of each nonprofit board serve on the congregation's governing board. The representative board member is meant to provide a communication link between governing bodies.

It is generally not effective to provide linkages between boards by requiring members of 501(c)(3) boards to sit on the congregation's governing board. This automatically places the crossover board member in a representational mindset. It also adds numbers to a board that needs to be kept small to effectively engage its strategic work. By design, representational members are serving on the board to promote the special interest of the organization they represent and not to represent the mission of the congregation. Their presence as a representative of the other board encourages a system of reporting and permission giving that tugs the governing body too heavily into management mode.

It is much better to build bridges between the boards through policy setting, goal setting, and sharing minutes and reports. Representatives from other boards can always be scheduled to attend a specific meeting to address evaluative and strategic questions, or to form strategic partnerships as needed.

In addition to 501(c)(3) boards, some large congregations operate with elder boards or program councils in addition to their governing board. This is often referred to as a bicameral system of governance. Inevitably, when a congregation operates with a multiple board system, questions emerge about how the multiple boards are supposed to work together. I must acknowledge my own bias here. I am not a fan of bicameral systems in the large congregation. I believe that they cloud strategic thinking and discourage the alignment of staff and board.

Let's examine the congregation that operates with a program council. This council supposedly exists to help coordinate and facilitate communication among the various ministry programs of the congregation. Once a congregation has entered the professional size category, this type of council no longer works effectively (if it ever did). The coordination of the ministries happens best in a weekly staff meeting. A program council that meets monthly isn't meeting frequently enough to provide the careful coordination needed in the large congregation. Furthermore, a program council involves laity in excessive administrative detail, instead of freeing them up to do hands-on ministry. Finally, it is difficult to figure out what the relationship is between the program council and the governing board. It blurs the distinction between governance and ministry that we so carefully explored using the Hotchkiss model.

Let's also consider the use of elder boards in large congregations. Some large congregations continue to operate with elder boards that are meant to oversee and protect the spiritual life of the congregation. Again, this creates an artificial dichotomy in leadership that is often detrimental to the large congregation. It suggests that those who provide governance leadership to the congregation are not capable of being spiritual individuals, or worse, that they are not responsible for being spiritual leaders because someone else is tending to the sacred side of leadership. Some elder boards function in a purely advisory capacity to senior clergy leaders. In this sense they are fairly harmless in the life of the congregation (although I've rarely encountered a senior clergy leader who finds their official presence as a board particularly helpful). At their worst, elder boards become hotbeds of opposition to the strategic leadership of the governing board. The key to functioning with a healthy elder board (if your polity or history requires that you function with one) is to clearly define a set of responsibilities for the elder board that engage it in meaningful strategic dialogue with the governing board. An elder board that has been sidelined with no meaningful work to do is likely to become a dysfunctional body that will invent its own form of dysfunctional work.

Designing an effective governance system for the large congregation is central to the health of all five leadership systems discussed in this book. The following discussion questions will help you and your leaders maximize the effectiveness of both the board and staff team. These questions will provide your leaders with shared terminology to dialogue about governance, which is the first step in building a strong and stable leadership system.

QUESTIONS FOR INDIVIDUAL OR GROUP REFLECTION

1. What practices is your board engaging in that support its strategic and generative work? What practices are detracting from its strategic and generative work? What might you change?

2. The Hotchkiss governance model makes a distinction between the governance or oversight work of the board, and the ministry management work of the staff team. In what ways is this distinction helpful for your context?

3. Does your board operate with an adequate set of policies, allowing it to appropriately delegate the management of the church to board committees and the staff team? What would you add to make your policies more complete?

4. How many people serve on the governing board in your congregation? Is your board an appropriately sized board to engage in strategic leadership? If not, what changes would you recommend in either board size or structure to make it more effective?

5. To what extent is the makeup of your board driven by a desire to mirror the demographics of the congregation? How is this helping or hurting board function?

6. Does your congregation have a personnel committee or human resource committee? If so, in what ways are the current practices of the committee helpful or hurtful to good governance?

EXERCISE ONE:
MAINTAINING THE RIGHT FOCUS

As a governing board struggles to find its place in the operational and strategic leadership of the congregation, it tends to move back and forth along three continuums. Think about the work of your own governing board over the past twelve months. Place an X on each of the three lines below to indicate the position your board has occupied on each scale.

Involvement in knowing, informing, and deciding on behalf of the congregation:

Little Involvement   Much Involvement

Relationship to the Staff Team

Under-Control   Effective Oversight   Over-Control

Orientation toward Time

Past Focus   Present Focus   Future Focus

1. Does the placement of your 'X' on these three continuums feel appropriate, given the size and complexity of your congregation? Should your governing board be moving toward more or less involvement, more or less control in its relationship with the staff team, and more or less focus on the past/present/future? Why?

2. What do the positions occupied by your governing board suggest about whether your board is focusing on strategic management, or strategic leadership? Where should the focus of your board be? What practices would you add or eliminate to better position your board?

CHAPTER 7

Acculturation and Engagement of the Laity

ANNA AND CURTIS HAVE BEEN AFFILIATED WITH UNITY CHURCH FOR NINE years. They are passionate about the congregation's ministry to the homeless and working poor. Over the years they have taken turns serving on the social justice ministry team and they have actively invested themselves in managing Recycled Treasures, a ministry aimed at distributing gently used clothing, toys, and household items to the economically disadvantaged.

During the course of Anna and Curtis's history with Unity Church, its weekend worshiping community has grown from 350 to 1,100. The congregation's ministry to the working poor has grown accordingly. The church has experienced many organizational growing pains over the years, but Anna and Curtis have been unfazed by this as they have happily and effectively led the ministry. They have made most of the decisions pertaining to the administration of Recycled Treasures over the years and have had the support of the staff team as needed. That is, until recently.

Sarah is the clergy leader who oversees the social justice ministry of the congregation. Recently, she has been evaluating how the congregation's various ministries to the economically disadvantaged in the community are working together. One point of tension has become increasingly obvious to her. Recycled Treasures traditionally engages in a large-scale donation of used clothing and toys during the month of December in an attempt to support the working poor during the holiday season. The congregation also

171

has a practice of providing Christmas gift baskets to community families in need. The baskets incorporate food, new clothing, and toys purchased with the specific needs of chosen families in mind. Both ministries require a significant investment of staff time in the month of December, and both require dedicated use of the same space in the church building. The two ministries tend to serve the same population.

Last month, Sarah made the decision to reschedule the Recycled Treasures distribution of clothing and toys from December to April, believing that both of the ministries as well as the client base that both ministries serve would be better served by the rescheduling. She appropriately worked the change in scheduling through the staff team and through the ministry team that supports social justice ministries. Both teams supported the schedule change, and Sarah informed Anna and Curtis about the change well in advance of their traditional gearing-up process for the December Recycled Treasures drive.

One week after Sarah informed Anna and Curtis about the scheduling change, the couple requested a meeting with the senior pastor of Unity. Walking into his office, Anna and Curtis submitted their resignations from Recycled Treasures and asked that their names be removed from the congregation's membership book. They expressed outrage that this ministry that had always been theirs to administer had suddenly been co-opted by a member of the staff team. In fact, Anna and Curtis thought that the leadership of the congregation had generally gotten very much off track. They observed that this used to be a congregation where the staff team served the volunteer leaders of the church as they engaged their ministry. The staff team would shape their time and attention in response to the leadership initiatives of the laity. Now it seemed that the efforts of the laity were being managed and directed by the staff team, and things were feeling very backwards and misguided. The pastor's efforts to explain how things needed to work in the size congregation that Unity had become were wasted on Anna and Curtis. They left his office and Unity Church on that day and never returned.

Whose Church Is It?

The disorientation that laity experience as a congregation moves out of the multi-celled size category and into the professional and strategic zones is palpable. Astute lay leaders will ask, "If the staff team is going to run the place, then what work is ours to do?" When faced with the transition from being a congregation that is managed by the laity to being one that is managed by the staff team, a variety of missteps can take place. Some congregations move into a mode of operation that treats the staff team like hired help, employed to do the ministry of the church on the congregation's behalf. This mindset results in a disengaged laity who see their role as executive directors and financiers of the work. Other congregations set up a dichotomy in which the members become watchdogs over the staff team, making certain that the staff team does not misuse its authority or the assets of the church. This approach also results in a laity that is disengaged from the active ministry of the congregation.

Healthy large congregations realize that the ministry of the church still belongs to the members, who must actively participate in the ministry. The staff team manages ministry efforts but does not do ministry on behalf of the laity. The members in the large congregation are active leaders, discerners, governors and ministry participants. Their involvement in decision making works differently in the large church than it does in the small to mid size congregation. This can cause those who come out of smaller church environments to feel less involved.

In the small and mid-size congregation, laity and clergy often sit in the room together to negotiate the management and leadership needs of the congregation. Board meetings and committee meetings are grounded in the managerial decisions that form the ministry. In fact, one of the critiques of church life in the mid-sized congregation is the amount of time that members spend on administration. One often hears laity express a longing to spend less time in the administration of ministry and more time in the actual doing of ministry.

Toward the upper end of the professional size category and moving into the strategic size category, the healthy congregation begins to experience a phenomenon that feels like the staff team is seizing control of the congregation. Decisions that used to be made by members are suddenly made by members of the staff team. Lay leaders often experience a sense of betrayal by their clergy leaders. Initially members may feel that the clergy leadership of the church is on some kind of power trip, trying to wrest control away from lay leadership. In fact, the clergy leaders are intuitively responding to the organizational needs of the church, a need for a different kind of decision making.

So, what is the role of laity in the large congregation? How do laypersons effectively engage in the decision making of the church? How does staff ensure that lay leaders continue to own the ministries of the church? I'll examine these questions and more in this chapter as we explore the involvement of the laity and the way in which acculturation works in the large congregation.

THE CENTRALITY OF LAY LEADERSHIP

Within the Christian tradition we often lift up 1 Corinthians 12 as a call to the ministry of the laity.

> There are different kinds of gifts, but the same Spirit distributes them. There are different kinds of service, but the same Lord. There are different kinds of working, but in all of them and in everyone it is the same God at work.
>
> Now to each one the manifestation of the Spirit is given for the common good. To one there is given through the Spirit a message of wisdom, to another a message of knowledge by means of the same Spirit, to another faith by the same Spirit, to another gifts of healing by that one Spirit, to another miraculous powers, to another prophecy, to another distinguishing between spirits, to another speaking in different kinds of tongues, and to still another the interpretation of tongues. All these are the work of one and the same Spirit, and he distributes them to each one, just as he determines. (1 Cor. 12:1–11 NIV)

When leaders grow confused about the role of the laity in the large congregation, arguments will be made that the church has lost its way and forgotten about the giftedness of the laity. In fact, nothing could be further from the truth. I believe that the giftedness of the laity is more acutely emphasized and valued in the large congregation, not less.

In the smaller congregation the strategic leadership, the strategic management, and the operational management of the church tend to happen interchangeably in a variety of meeting venues. Board meetings, committee meetings and staff meetings all incorporate dialogue in all three arenas, sometimes within a single meeting. The blending of all forms of leadership and management, with lay leaders in the room and involved in the debate, means that laity is fully integrated into the decision-making life of the congregation. The downside of this type of integrated decision making is that people often feel that their personal giftedness is not being used to its fullest. Some long to be released from the administration of the ministry, so they can engage in more hands on ministry. "I just want to sing, or teach the kids, or serve the homeless. I don't want to attend all of these meetings."

As a church grows larger, the complexity of the congregation grows. There is an increasing need for professionalism in the ministry and for coordination across areas of ministry. Strategic leadership, strategic management, and operational management can no longer happen in the same place. Decision-making authority starts getting parceled out to the governing board, staff team, and committees of the congregation. The governing board becomes more strategic in its focus, delegating the operational management of the church to the staff team. (See chapter 6, "Governance and Board Structure," for a more complete description of which leadership bodies need to adopt which type of work.)

The result of these shifts in organization, and the resulting changes in the distribution of authority, means that lay leaders are often no longer in the room when key operational decisions are being made. So those who don't want to attend so many meetings are happy, but others may feel left out. For some, this change creates the feeling that the church is being hijacked by the staff team and that the role of laity has been diminished. In fact, the redistribution of decision-making authority has the capacity to engage the

giftedness of the laity more fully than the system in which everyone makes all the decisions together. When lay leaders are freed
from the operational decision making that is taken over by the
staff team, they are also freed to more fully engage the ministerial
areas in which they are gifted. Those who are good at the tasks
of governance serve as board leaders. Those with passionate and
creative ideas about the various ministries of the church serve on
ministry teams and work alongside staff leaders to shape those
ministries. Those with particular gifts for teaching invest themselves more fully in the tasks of teaching . . . and so on. As the staff
team becomes more professionalized and specialized, the work of
the laity also becomes more specialized, with each person working
more exclusively in his or her own area of giftedness.

Some of the changes associated with these shifts will register
as losses to leaders who've been intimately engaged in the life of
the congregation, people like Anna and Curtis in the story that
opened this chapter. When a congregation goes through this kind
of transition, intentional work must be done with lay leaders to
help them understand how their voices can be used to influence
decision making, if they so desire.

In the large congregation, proportionately fewer people make
decisions than in the small congregation. The staff team is larger,
the board is smaller, and a relatively small group of lay leaders
are actually making decisions on behalf of the congregation. In
the large church, those lay leaders who make decisions in particular areas of ministry are rarely aware of decision making in other
areas of ministry. Even board leaders (if they are focusing on the
strategic leadership of the congregation) are not aware of decisions
made in specific programming areas. You have to be an upper-level
manager on the staff team in the very large church to have inside
working knowledge about decisions being made around the entire
church. This adds to the feeling that lay leaders have "lost the
church."

In fact, if lay leaders are living into their role, then they are full
owners of the mission, discerners of next steps, strategic direction
setters, ministry managers alongside the staff, and doers of the
ministry. Let's look at how each of these roles is played in the large
congregation.

Mission Owners

Denominational polities hold different assumptions about who "owns" the church. However, most mainline Protestant congregations believe that the laity has an ownership voice in the strategic direction of the congregation. Regardless of who owns the building and who can hire or fire clergy leaders, most traditions appreciate that the strategic direction of the church is vested in the members of the congregation. At the beginning and end of the day, it is the membership body that must affirm the vision, core values, and strategic priorities of the congregation. If the laity doesn't affirm the direction of the congregation, no board or staff team can steer the congregation.

In the large congregation the articulation and affirmation of strategy works very much like it does in the smaller congregation. Good strategic questions are framed about the identity of the congregation, and data is gathered to help formulate answers to those questions. Leaders make meaning out of the data that has been gathered and then envision a preferred future.

However, over the years Alban consultants have noticed something remarkable in how congregations of all sizes pursue mission ownership. The leadership body that invests itself in the articulation of mission and vision is typically a group of 75 to 100 leaders. Whether the congregation is multi-celled, professional, strategic, or matrix in size, when an open call is issued to the "leaders of the congregation" about 75 leaders will show up. Upwards of 1,000 members may participate in individual acts of discernment (like participating in a survey or listening group), but those who will engage in collective decision making on behalf of the congregation number between 75 and 100 leaders.

When 75 leaders show up to participate in the decision making of a congregation that averages 150 people in weekend attendance, leaders think that people are engaged. When 75 leaders show up to make decisions for a congregation with 1,200 in worship, leaders think that members have yielded their ownership of the church. This often frustrates those who believe that a larger body of people should be investing in the leadership of the congregation.

This group of 75 to 100 individuals behaves remarkably like the community-size group discussed in chapter 2. This is the group size that can effectively function as a community with a leadership identity. The leaders are sorting themselves into a manageable body of thinkers who are equipped to do this work on the congregation's behalf. Members are not necessarily bailing on their investment in the church. It is a sign that people intuitively know that some people are gifted for more strategic decision making, and some are gifted for more operational or hands-on forms of ministry. The laity is sorting itself according to the work that they do best.

Discerners

Discernment about the mission and ministry of the congregation is happening at all times and in every venue of large church leadership. Lay leaders never need to abdicate their role as discerners of God's movement in the ministry, regardless of church size. What differs across size categories is the arena in which discernment happens. In the large church there are few open forums where members can show up and weigh in on whatever issue may be burdening their hearts. In smaller churches congregational meetings and board meetings are often open meetings, where members can show up to talk about anything they feel compelled to address. Someone in the small or mid-size congregation who is feeling led to express an opinion has easy access to decision makers. In the larger congregation, as we have already seen, decision making is happening in more specialized arenas.

In the large congregation, showing up at an all church meeting to express a random opinion about the budget is no longer helpful behavior. Directions have been so well established by the time a congregational meeting occurs that voting is almost always a vote of affirmation and an expression of support for leadership. A "member at large" is not necessarily encouraged to show up at a governing board meeting to share his inspiration or concern around a particular area of ministry. If board leaders are healthy, the board is working at a strategic level and would refer a conversation about an operating concern to an appropriate ministry team of the church.

Discerning lay leaders in the large congregation have to be politically savvy enough to understand when and where to register their ideas. They need to share their impressions, hopes, and dreams with the appropriate staff member, or they need to bring those thoughts to the appropriate ministry team for further exploration. Discernment is still very much a part of the role of lay leaders, but the delivery system needs to be thoughtfully targeted if it is going to have impact.

Ministry Managers

The management of ministry in the large church is primarily coordinated by the staff team. However, the staff team does not fulfill the management function alone. Ministry teams of lay leaders come alongside staff members to help shape and coordinate ministry. Ministry teams exist in all size congregations. What is distinct in the large congregation is the role that staff leaders play in shaping the team.

In the large church, staff members often know best who is passionate about and gifted for various areas of ministry. The large church may function with a lay leadership group that officially nominates people to serve on its various committees and teams. However, the staff of the church will have significant input into the nomination process. The effective large congregation yields much of the decision making about individual areas of ministry to staff members, who work carefully in concert with appointed lay leaders to shape the ministry. Ministry teams in the large church understand that they will be most effective when staff coordinates volunteers, not when the volunteers try to coordinate staff.

Ministers

One of the things that first attracted me to my own home congregation was a section at the bottom of the weekly bulletin that listed the various staff roles of the church. For each role the title of the position was listed, and next to the title was the name of the person occupying the role. At the bottom of the list it said: "Ministers: Every member of the congregation."

I am an American Baptist, and the notion that every member of the congregation is responsible for his or her own relationship with God and for ministry of the church is part of my DNA. Most Protestant congregations operate with some sense of this same notion. The large church is no different from the small church in this regard. A staff team of 25 individuals, or even 50 individuals, cannot accomplish in ministry what an orchestrated group of 800 to 1,000 members can accomplish. Lay leaders are "doers" of ministry when they sing in worship, teach a religious education class, lead a small group, serve a meal to the homeless, donate items to the food pantry, and so forth. You get the picture.

HOW PEOPLE BECOME CONNECTED

In *The Tipping Point* author Malcolm Gladwell writes about the people who link us up with the rest of the world. He calls these individuals *connectors*, people with a special gift for bringing the world together. Connectors are people who know many others and can quickly build relationships between people, because they manage to occupy many different worlds and subcultures and niches at once.[1]

Faith communities have long relied upon connectors to manage the assimilation of newcomers. The apostle Paul was a connector, building relationships within and between Jewish communities around the Mediterranean that were embracing the teachings of Jesus Christ. Through his letters he created a network of faith communities that understood their connection to one another, even if they didn't personally interact with one another.

Congregations of all sizes rely upon connectors to build relationships among members, to connect new people to existing congregational groups, and to ensure that people know one another. You can spot congregational connectors from a distance just by observing the way they gravitate toward newcomers, move during a meet-and-greet period, and physically bring people together.

In the effective large congregation connectors are found in different roles than they are found in small and mid-sized congregations. Arlin Rothauge first identified the ways in which different size congregations assimilate new members in his pamphlet "Sizing Up a Congregation for New Member Ministry."[2] Rothauge identified that in the small, family-size congregation (0–50 in average weekly worship attendance), the matriarch or patriarch of the congregation makes the connections. In the pastoral-size congregation (50–150), the pastor is the most effective connector. In the program-size church (150–350), the various department chairs and staff members who oversee programs collectively share the connecting function, spotting newcomers and connecting them to programs and people.

In the professional size congregation, the connecting work is most effective when done by the staff team, where it is often coordinated via the weekly staff meeting. The congregation has grown beyond the capacity of any one individual to know and be known by everyone. If the senior clergy person has been in place for a long time and the congregation has grown up around her, she may demonstrate a remarkable capacity to know people. However, it is still the collective staff team that provides the connecting function for the congregation.

Each professional leader on the staff team is responsible for connecting those active participants most closely associated with his or her area of ministry. The youth leader and children's leader may collaboratively track and connect families with school-aged children. The senior adult minister tracks and connects those in the congregation over the age of 65. The music minister connects those who serve the congregation through music. In this manner the professional church manages to keep tabs on its membership. There may be areas of overlap, and occasionally a person falls through the cracks because the person doesn't fit any particular interest or involvement group. The entire system of connection in this size congregation is dependent upon the coordinating capabilities of the staff team.

Once a congregation passes into the strategic size category, the capacity of the staff team to serve in a connecting capacity is seriously diminished. Too many people begin falling through the cracks. The size of individual ministries may pass the Dunbar number of 150, the number of people that any one leader can reasonably track. (See chapter 2 for further explanation.) Too many participants in the life of the congregation don't fall into the neat classification system formed by staff member ministries. Earlier methods for recruiting people for ministry suddenly quit working. In short, the connection system that has been so adroitly managed by the staff team begins to fail.

In this size category the staff team continues to serve as connectors, but individual staff members become painfully aware that their efforts to connect people are inadequate. When a congregation hits this limit, it needs to begin thinking more systematically about the connection process. The strategic church and the matrix church both recognize that leaders must create a seamless system of acculturation, one that invites every member of the congregation to participate in the connection process. The culture of the congregation must encourage every member to feel responsible for the welcoming and acculturation of others. The process for assimilating into the life of the congregation, and eventually for some to enter into the leadership life of the congregation, must become so transparent that new people can take responsibility for their own integration.

ASSIMILATION VS. ACCULTURATION

In the 1980s literature and workshops about assimilating new members became the rage in church circles. People were asking, "Why are attendance and membership numbers showing such rapid decline?" Leaders were convinced that better systems of inviting, welcoming, and incorporating new participants into the life of the congregation were a key strategy for reversing declining membership and attendance patterns. Today you'd be hard pressed to find a workshop on new member assimilation. The center of the conversation has shifted, as has the way that we talk about receiving and incorporating newcomers.

In 1988, author Robert Bast identified assimilation as having three components: absorption, integration, and incorporation.[3]

Assimilation was understood to be the means by which a congregation coordinated and blended new members into a meaningful and unified whole. Pastor and author Owen Facey defined *assimilation* as an ongoing process of intentionally bringing, including, and integrating people into the life of the local church, with the goal of equipping and releasing them to serve.[4]

In the 1990s people began to rethink the language of assimilation. As the culture in the United States became more pluralistic and more ethnically, racially, and socially diverse, people began to question whether it was appropriate to use the term *assimilation* in corporate and business settings. Leading thinkers argued that the term *assimilation* had an inappropriate "melting pot" quality that didn't appropriately honor the welcome differences that newcomers might bring. Assimilation suggests one-way adaptation, in which the newcomer assumes the cultural norms of the dominant group. The dominant culture of the congregation is not expected to accommodate any of the unique attributes that the newcomer brings.[5]

Acculturation is a broader concept that more appropriately recognizes the need for both the organization and the individual to mutually adapt to one another. Acculturation is a two-way process of integration in which both culture groups (the congregation and the individual) change to some degree to accommodate the norms and values of one other.[6]

I believe that when we talk about the integration of new members into a large congregation, we need to embrace the language of acculturation, not assimilation. First, it is a more appropriate way of thinking for many of our congregations, those struggling to diversify membership. If we truly want to welcome members who look and think differently from the people already sitting in the pews, then we need to think about new-member integration as a mutual process of acculturation.

Second, one of the strengths of the large congregation is its ability to accommodate greater diversity. People can find others with whom they identify, without the entire congregation having to negotiate every difference in the community all the time. Those who are uncomfortable with difference can avoid it by distancing themselves from the "other." And those who embrace diversity can find the difference they seek. When people join the large congregation, they don't really join the whole church; they join that portion of the church with which they identify. This makes room for diverse viewpoints and interests to live comfortably side by side. If we want to cultivate a culture that embraces diversity, then we need to view the integration of new members through the lens of acculturation, not assimilation.

This change in perspective ought to have significant ramifications for the way in which we approach the integration of newcomers. What might our welcoming, orienting, and membership processes look like if we are intentionally trying to adapt to each newcomer who arrives?

SHIFTING ENTRY POINTS

Traditionally, worship has been regarded as the primary venue through which individuals enter the life of a congregation. In *The Inviting Church,* Alban consultants' Roy Oswald and Speed Leas linked new-member assimilation with spiritual growth. They named six levels of incorporation into the spiritual life of the church that progressed in this order: joining, belonging, participating, searching, journeying inward, and journeying outward. Oswald and Leas were careful to explain that individuals might not progress through the six stages in linear fashion. In fact, they argued that the first three steps may be disassociated from the last three. But they nevertheless assumed that people begin their engagement with the church through worship and then move through deeper levels of involvement from there. Here is how they described the progression:

> When people are in the process of choosing and joining a congregation, they "get active" in certain ways. They are curious and they begin to explore. They go to church first to worship; they begin to talk with members about their experience at the church; they take inquirers classes, orientation classes, or confirmation classes; and sometimes they get involved in other ongoing church

classes or programs to find out what these folks believe, what people who are members here do. . . .

We found that as members "get in" to the church (this may well be before they formally join the congregation) their needs for belonging and inclusion become stronger than their curiosities and faith questions. After people feel that they have "gotten in," this is usually after having formally joined the church) they look for ways to belong. . . .

Some members move into another phase of involvement (which may not decrease their belonging activities) we call Participation This is a busier kind of taking part. Here people don't just respond when asked, they take initiative. They notice when things need doing and they do what is required. They are most likely on a board or committee, teaching a class, and/or in a position of trust with regard to the church books, money raising, or making sure that church is heated for Sunday morning worship."[7]

A lot has changed in congregational and mainstream culture since Oswald and Leas wrote about assimilation. People have shifted the way that they integrate into congregations. Joining is rarely the first step and may not even enter into the equation. Some would argue that the first three steps today are actually a reversal of the process described above, particularly among the millennial generation. People's involvement is more likely to follow this path: participating, belonging, and then joining.

Some new arrivals at the church begin by participating in the outreach or service opportunities the congregation sponsors. They move from participation into a quest for deeper belonging, where they test out small group involvement or worship, and finally they move toward joining, taking orientation and membership classes much later in their church experience.

This reversal in assimilation patterns is particularly evident in the large church. While many continue to treat weekend worship as the center of church life, others do not. The large church offers so many programming options that Sunday morning worship is no longer the only feeder system of the church. People who are attached to the church school, a fine arts program, or a recovery program or support group may not be particularly drawn to weekend worship. Nevertheless, these people believe that they are active participants in the life of the church, and they expect that the community will care for them, educate them, and tend to their spiritual needs. They think of whatever pastor they have the most intimate contact with as "their" pastor, and their pastor may actually have minimal involvement in leading worship. They may not be formal members of the church, but they often describe the church as their own.

This phenomenon introduces a number of interesting challenges into the congregation's acculturation process. In the 1980s our best guess for how to assimilate new members centered almost entirely on Sunday morning worship. We obsessed over the availability of parking and the training of our greeters, ushers, and welcome-table hosts. We tracked participation in worship services and mailed a carefully conceived series of follow-up letters that drew people ever more deeply into the life of the congregation.

For many newcomers, worship remains the primary entry point, and so all those things we worried about back in the '80s are still relevant. However, if people are not regularly attending Sunday worship, then we need to have integration systems in place that will gather in those who are participating less traditionally. Every ministry of the church needs to have its own method for drawing people more deeply into the life of the congregation. Critical incidents or trigger points need to be identified for flagging people who are expressing an interest in the life of the congregation outside of worship.

CREATING A CULTURE OF ENGAGEMENT

The larger a congregation becomes, the more that it needs to build a culture of engagement, an environment in which every member embraces her part in the welcome and acculturation of new members. Additionally, the overall process for becoming connected to the congregation must be transparent to newcomers, so they can take some measure of responsibility for their own engagement.

Methodist bishop Robert Schnase refers to "Radical Hospitality" as one of the Five Practices of Fruitful Congregations. Radical Hospitality exists when, out of genuine love for God and others, laity and clergy take the initiative to invite, welcome, include, and support newcomers and help them grow into their affiliation with the body. Members focus on those outside of their congregation with as much passion as they attend to the nurture and growth of those who already belong to the family, and they apply their utmost creativity, energy, and effectiveness to the task.[8]

Congregations practicing Radical Hospitality offer surprising and unexpected depth and authenticity in their caring for the stranger. Newcomers intuitively sense this. Churches marked by this quality work hard to figure out how best to anticipate others' needs and to make them feel at home in their ministries. Members work with heightened awareness of the person who is not present or who is present for the first time.

Creating a culture of engagement is no easy task. Organizational development pioneer Edgar Schein identified three distinct levels of an organization that must be addressed to genuinely create and sustain a new culture. A congregation that seeks to embrace Radical Hospitality needs to tend simultaneously to all three of these layers.[9]

Figure 7.1 Levels of Culture

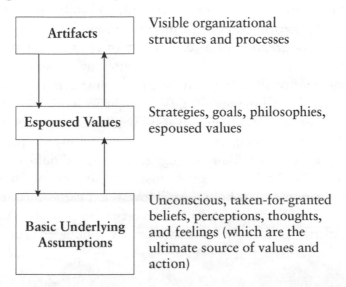

Nearest to the surface of the culture are the artifacts. These are the collective phenomena that a newcomer might see, hear, or feel when encountering the congregation. These include things like the accessibility of the welcome center, the presence of the usher team, the layout of the parking lot, the attractiveness and clarity of welcome brochures, adequacy of signage in the building, whether members wear nametags, whether they are greeted by the pastor, and the like. A series of classes (perhaps as basic as Membership 101, 201, and 301) are offered frequently in an easy-to-access format. Many congregations tend to these important features, but they mistakenly assume that these artifacts alone are enough to create a welcoming culture. They are not.

An engaging culture must also be reflected at the next deepest level, which is where the espoused values of the congregation reside. A congregation must have a clearly articulated belief system, teaching members why they should feel compelled to welcome the newcomer. Each member should be able to answer these questions. What does my engagement of the newcomer have to do with my own spiritual journey? What is the congregation's philosophy about my role in welcoming and engaging the newcomer? How does it benefit me, the congregation, and the newcomer? The average person in the pew needs to be exposed frequently to the congregation's message about acculturation. Members need to hear it from the pulpit, in congregational correspondence, within small groups, in board and committee meetings, and so forth. The message must be consistent, unified, and ubiquitous.

Finally, the creation of a real culture of engagement requires work at the deepest level where subconscious thought resides. Every member of the congregation carries unstated assumptions in his head about how acculturation ought to work. For example: "If the pastor were doing his job I wouldn't need to do this." Or, "It's up to newcomers to approach me with any questions they may have. I'm willing to engage but they should take the first step." These beliefs are often unspoken, and people may not even be aware that they hold them. However, it is the unstated assumptions at work in the life of the congregation that often undermine leadership efforts to create a more welcoming environment.

A congregation may have an impressive lineup of organizational structures and processes to tend to the newcomer. The congregation may have clearly articulated strategies, goals, values, and philosophies about the work of engagement belonging to the entire congregation. But, if the person sitting in the pew believes, at the core of his being, that the job of acculturation belongs to the staff team of the church, all the other efforts will be wasted. If members believe that "newcomers ought to be able to figure out how to engage on their own, because after all, that is the way that I did it when I first arrived," there is no culture of engagement. Each member must operate with a set of underlying assumptions that supports her involvement in Radical Hospitality, in reaching out to the other.

A culture is truly in place only once the artifacts, espoused values, and basic underlying assumptions of the congregation are in alignment. How does this happen? It happens when leaders work consistently, over a long period of time, on all three levels of the culture. While new processes and structures are being designed, people are being invited to explore their own unstated assumptions about engagement. While the governing board is working on strategies, goals, and philosophies, members are being invited to consider their role in creating a more inclusive and inviting environment.

Staff Positions That Help

Two staff positions that emerge in large congregations are critical for creating and tending a culture of engagement. These positions are the director of communications and the director of membership. They may operate under different names, but their purpose is relatively stable across congregations.

The communications role typically begins as a part-time role in the professional size congregations. It becomes a full-time position in the strategic congregation. In the matrix size church the director of communications often supervises a team of staff dedicated to the communication and public relations function of the congregation.

The need for clear and consistent branding and messaging in the large church is readily apparent. Often the role originates with someone who is asked to coordinate the weekly electronic newsletter and worship bulletin. At some point it becomes imperative to coordinate the messages of those important communication venues with the congregation's website, the pastors' blogs, program flyers, and so forth. The larger the congregation becomes, the more important it is to have an overarching branding and messaging system to communicate a focused and consistent message.

The director of communication can play a significant role in the creation of a culture of engagement. Each of the communication venues of the congregation is an important opportunity to influence the culture on all three levels described above. Communication channels can be employed to help people figure out where to get connected and how to learn more about the congregation. The website becomes a vehicle for interacting with the congregation. People can find out what is happening on the website, and they can sign up to participate in various ways through the website. They can listen to sermons that they missed, and they can register their feelings and perceptions through interactive surveys and data-gathering tools. The publications of the congregation provide the information that people need to make intelligent choices about their own participation. All the communication venues of the congregation can be used to repeat and inculcate the congregation's basic values.

The other staff team role that becomes increasingly critical to the effectiveness of the large church is the director of membership. This role focuses on the welcome and acculturation of newcomers and is often tied to the stewardship and leadership development focus of the congregation. The way in which the role is constructed varies considerably from one congregation to the next.

When the role first emerges, it is almost always placed on the administrative side of the staff team, and it is almost always staffed part-time. The staff member spends most of her time developing a reporting system to track participation and membership and to better manage the welcoming function at weekend worship. The position is usually staffed by a lay member of the congregation who knows a lot of people and cares about the mission of the congregation. As the congregation continues to grow past the 800 mark, the demands on the staff member become more significant and a greater level of professionalization is required. A more sophisticated program of acculturation must be developed that can guide the footsteps of a first-time visitor from the first point of entry until he is a fully engaged member. In the very large church the person in this role is responsible for the welcoming function, membership classes, and connecting people into meaningful volunteer opportunities. Sometimes the director of membership is housed under the pastoral care arm of the staff team. Sometimes it is treated as part of the discipleship function, and sometimes it is treated as part of a development or stewardship group. The larger the congregation, the less administrative and the more programmatic the role becomes.

In many of the large congregations I've worked in, both the director of communication and the director of membership suffer from an identity crisis. They wonder where they fit on the staff team and exactly what they are meant to be doing. The lack of clarity creates a great deal of conflict (and resulting stress) for the occupants of the role. In fact, the occupants of both positions usually straddle the program and administrative support teams. They must be able to function and move easily as members of both teams.

From a distance, the large congregation may appear to be a place of anonymity and disengagement. The perception may be that people join the large church to hide, and the staff team does ministry on behalf of the laity. In this chapter I have attempted to dispel that myth. The large congregation will always house a body of people who have selected the congregation specifically because of their desire to remain anonymous. But alongside that anonymous body of people is a significant cadre of laity who are working to support the congregation in highly engaged and specialized ways. In the effective large congregation, the staff team knows that they do not exist to carry out ministry on behalf of laity. The staff knows they exist to equip laity in the pursuit of the congregation's mission. In the next chapter we will examine the process of forming and executing the congregation's mission, in a way that fully involves clergy, staff, and laity.

QUESTIONS FOR INDIVIDUAL OR GROUP REFLECTION

1. Think about the involvement of the laity in your own congregation. What are the ways in which the laity of your congregation can express their identity as missional owners, discerners, governors, ministry managers, and ministry participants?

2. Are there areas of your congregation where the laity is excluded from leadership? Is this appropriate or inappropriate, healthy or unhealthy, given the size of your congregation?

3. Connectors are people who know many others and build relationships between others quickly because they manage to occupy many different worlds, subcultures, and niches. Who are the connectors in your congregation? Who are the connectors on your staff team? Are your connectors empowered to facilitate the acculturation of new members? If not, what stands in their way?

4. Does the orientation of newcomers in your congregation focus on assimilation or acculturation?

5. What are the points of entry into life in your congregation, other than worship? Do your methods of welcoming and tracking newcomers take into consideration points of entry other than weekend worship?

6. This chapter identified three levels of culture that must be tended to create a welcoming congregation. What is your congregation currently doing to create a culture of engagement at the level of visible artifacts, at the level of espoused values, and at the level of basic underlying assumptions?

CHAPTER 8

Forming and Executing Strategy

WHAT MINISTRY IS UNIQUELY OURS TO DO, AND HOW DO WE STAY FOCUSED on it? This question targets the heart of a congregation's strategic identity. How are we different from any other congregation based on our ministry context, the passion and giftedness of our membership, and what God is calling us to do or become?

A congregation with a strong strategic identity is able to form an effective overall strategy for ministry. A well-formed strategy generally includes a narrative of core identity (or vision statement), a defined set of core values, an understanding of what strengths the congregation seeks to preserve, and two or three agreed-upon areas of new growth. When good strategic leadership is present, the congregation consistently acts in ways that demonstrate the core values, ministers to the community out of the congregation's strengths, and pursues growth in agreed upon areas.

The leadership system that tends to strategy is not as neatly defined as the other four leadership systems that have been discussed in prior chapters. The congregation's strategy must be embodied at every level of church life—in its clergy leaders, on the staff team, among board members, and in the assimilation of new members. Consequently, it is fitting that we visit this leadership system last. In many ways the formation and execution of strategy is the leadership system that brings all of the other leadership systems into alignment.

Strategic leadership is not the responsibility of a single person. Congregations would often like to pin responsibility for good strategic leadership on the shoulders of the senior clergy person or the board chairperson. It's true that I've rarely seen a congregation demonstrate good strategic leadership without effective strategic leadership from the senior clergy leader and board chair. On the other hand, I've seen many congregations sabotage strategically effective leaders at the top by choosing to ignore strategy at other leadership levels. The effectiveness of the senior clergy person and the board leader can only go so far in implementing the strategy of the congregation, if the remainder of the congregation ignores that direction.

In this chapter we will examine the mission identity of a congregation, the way in which strategy is formed, and how strategy is managed and led. We'll explore the interface between strategy formation and strategy execution. We'll examine the complexities of tending to strategy in larger congregations. But first, let's begin with a brief case study that illustrates the essential components of strategic leadership.

A TALE OF TWO CHURCHES

Crossroads Community Church and First Baptist are two congregations that claim Main Street as their home in an inner-ring suburb. The two congregations have rich individual stories and perhaps a shared future story.

Crossroads is a nondenominational nine-year-old congregation with 425 people in average worship attendance and very few members over the age of 40. The congregation doesn't yet own permanent worship space. It has operated from at least eight different locations in its young life, ranging from school auditoriums and cafeterias to a local music theatre. Interestingly, the congregation thinks of itself as the church at Fourth and Main, even though none of its varied worship sites have ever been on Main Street or Fourth Street, and there is no church building at Fourth and Main. The identity of Crossroads is steeped in the demographic characteristics of the people represented by the intersection of Fourth and

Main, up-and-coming 25- to 34-year-old professionals, just beginning their families, with an edgy bent towards the arts.

Crossroads is currently piloted by its second lead pastor, their founding pastor having returned to the parent church several years ago. Despite having changed locations eight times, having changed pastoral leadership, and having no denominational affiliation, the congregation has a remarkably clear identity. Crossroads exists to invite people to follow Jesus together. Their vision is to become a voice of hope in the metropolitan area they serve by communicating the message of Jesus in creative and tangible ways. They operate with six clearly defined core values:

- **Every Person Matters.** Each person is created in the image of God and entrusted with creative and spiritual gifts. Each is called upon to make a unique and humble contribution.
- **Taking the Next Step.** Becoming disciples of Jesus Christ requires faithfulness to Scripture and the leading of the Holy Spirit. The journey has to begin somewhere; it is an ongoing pilgrimage that begins where we are.
- **Authentic Community.** We seek to be a people that God might dwell among—open, honest, accepting, welcoming, and nonjudgmental. We recognize that we are better together than apart.
- **All of Life Is Worship.** God is good. In response to God's faithfulness we are compelled to respond with worship, reverence, and praise. Opportunities for worship exist in all areas of our lives; in work, play, study, prayer, giving, and service.
- **Love in Action.** God loves people and so we love people. We show God's love to the world through action born of compassion. Avoiding judgment, we seek to embody the love of Jesus Christ through tangible acts of kindness, care and service to others.
- **Sending Out.** We send empowered and equipped disciples of Jesus Christ into the world. All members are missionaries in the communities where they live, work, serve, and play.

The pastoral staff incorporates these core values into all of their teaching and into daily decision making. They host a worship service that is simple in format, incorporating praise and teaching elements, and focused on creating authentic connections between people and God. Crossroads leaders love the community represented by Fourth and Main. They love it so much that they have been drawn into relationship with First Baptist, because of the location of the First Baptist building and the fact that First Baptist has office and classroom space that Crossroads sorely needs.

First Baptist is a 175-year-old faith community that occupies a large facility located at the intersection of Main and First Streets. In its glory days (the 1960s) the church would pack in over 500 people on an average Sunday. Today the average attendance is around 85 people, and the median age of the congregation is probably 65. If you ask the people of First Baptist what is unique about their congregation, they will tell you some version of this response: "We are a family, a congregation that feels like a family. We are invested in mission, both in our community and abroad. We have always existed to serve families in the community that want to ground their children in faith." Then they will go on to say:

> But our children have all been raised in the faith and are gone. There are no more young families to tend. We love and care for one another and want to welcome others to become part of our ministry. Some time ago the community around us changed, and the people who live around Main Street today don't seem interested in church anymore—at least not church the way that we do it. We don't recognize this community any more. Our school systems are shrinking, and the downtown area is overrun with motorcycles and edgy boutique storefronts that cater to the kind of people who wear tattoos and body piercings. We have a beautiful worship space, a phenomenal organist/pianist, and a decent choir for a church our size. We care about the homeless, but frankly we're getting too old and tired to do much active ministry with the homeless any more. We love our pastor and our pastor loves us. We don't understand why people aren't attracted to us and this space.

Over the years First Baptist has made multiple efforts to get clearer about its identity, its ministry setting, and it future course. At least three major planning initiatives have been carried out in the last 15 years. The first initiative was a comprehensive year-long process that involved an outside consultant, writing a mission statement, and creating eight broad goals. The church reorganized its board and governance structure in the wake of the strategic plan and celebrated the new initiatives with great enthusiasm, but little happened. The pastor left. The new initiatives were not executed, and nothing changed. The church continued to decline. After a change in pastors (two changes, actually), the church tried again. In the next planning go-round, congregational leaders simply named specific action steps they were going to take to revitalize the church and its ministry. A few weak attempts at implementing the plans were met with mild resistance and then abandoned. Finally, the church engaged in serious conversations about the viability of its future and decided with great celebration to become a missional church, with a new outward orientation. As you might have guessed, nothing happened. Sadly, First Baptist can no longer afford both its building and its barebones staff team. The pastor is retiring at the end of the year. They need to make a decision this year about whether they will close the church, sell the building and move, or merge with another congregation.

Enter Crossroads. Crossroads and First Baptist began conversations two years ago about the use of the building at First and Main. Crossroads rents office space from First Baptist and is considering moving its worship space into the First Baptist building as well. Members of Crossroads are drawn to the rich traditional feeling of the building, because their worship invokes a strong sense of the sacred. The relationship between the congregations has slowly been built, and today the two faith communities are considering various forms of merger.

What has been happening with Crossroads and First Baptist is happening to churches on Main Street all across the country. The decline of the modern church and the rise of the postmodern church are being debated, discussed, written about, and analyzed by others with far more wisdom about the church than I. I won't presume to oversimplify the journeys of these two congregations or to attribute the rise of Crossroads and the decline of First Baptist to a few easily articulated principles. The issues are much too complex to boil down to a few generalizations. However, I would like to examine one specific aspect of leadership in these two congregations to illustrate how two very different approaches have birthed different outcomes. I'd like to examine the journeys of Crossroads and First Baptist strictly through the lens of strategic leadership— not the leadership of the senior pastors (in fact, I'd like to leave the pastors out of it at this point), but the overall organizational strategy of each congregation.

First Baptist has struggled with issues of strategic leadership for at least 20 years. The congregation has never clearly articulated who it is or what is unique about its ministry. In each of the strategic planning efforts, congregational leaders wrote mission statements that were so broad they indicated the church's firm desire to be all things to all people (both inside and outside of the congregation). None of the planning efforts in the congregation produced clear priorities that demonstrated awareness about what was unique about First Baptist in this community at this time. Because of this, the congregation has never had a firm basis for saying no to any initiative, other than claiming the absence of funding. Because the congregation can't say a firm no, it also can't claim a firm yes. Budget and time constraints always prohibit the church from being all that it dreams about, so congregational leaders settle into maintaining the status quo, rather than risking offending a current member or by moving in a direction that isn't fully embraced by every person who calls the church home. In fairness to First Baptist, it is extremely difficult for a congregation with a 175-year journey to claim a strategic identity that fully honors both its history and its present membership and shapes the future . . . all at the same time.

From its inception, Crossroads has been remarkably clear about its identity and the context it seeks to serve. It makes no apologies for who it is and understands that not everyone will be attracted to this particular ministry. Congregational leaders are active discerners. When the congregation is faced with hard, direction-changing decisions, they pray, they revisit their core values, and they frame their options in accordance with key identity statements. Then they act in a manner that is consistent with their core identity. As they execute plans, they learn about their environment and make course corrections. They check progress, measure results, evaluate where they are headed, and reshape their next steps accordingly. In short, Crossroads exhibits good strategic leadership.

STRATEGIC LEADERSHIP DEFINED

When asked to define *worship* or *beauty*, people struggle to come up with words that are universally descriptive and that capture the full essence of the thing. So it is with *strategic leadership*. You know it when you are experiencing it, and you most certainly recognize when it's missing, but it is challenging to describe exactly what the thing is.

I'd like to propose a definition for strategic leadership in congregations, adapted from a definition of the term in *Becoming a Strategic Leader* by Richard Hughes and Katherine Beatty, senior associates at the Center for Creative Leadership.[1]

> Strategic leadership is the ability to think, act, and influence in ways that promote sustainable focus on the congregation's unique mission.

Strategic leadership is not just about planning. A congregation can assemble a phenomenal strategic plan that defines its identity and creates action steps but still be poor at strategic leadership. In fact, a question I am frequently asked by congregations beginning a strategic planning process is this: "What do we have to do to make certain that we actually execute this plan? We've created plans like this before and they simply sit there. They never come to fruition. Why is that?" The answer: The formation of strategy is only half of the equation. A congregation that doesn't have a good plan doesn't have much hope of sustaining focus, but the presence of a good plan is not enough to ensure that effective strategic leadership will occur. Leaders at all levels in the congregation must embrace the plan, choosing behaviors and implementing action steps in accordance with the priorities established in the plan.

Strategic leadership is not a project; it is a journey. A congregation can't participate in a strategic conversation for an intense period of time and then be done with strategic planning. Good strategic leadership is never-ending, always seeking to keep the membership body focused on and acting out of three critical identity questions: Who are we? Who is our neighbor? What is God calling us to do or become?[2] As action plans are implemented, those plans are evaluated and continually revised based on feedback from the environment.

Strategic leadership is about sustainability of thought, action, and influence, at every level of the congregation. Senior clergy, staff team, governing board, and committees all operate with the same set of priorities. Those priorities and the core values are consistently considered in every decision of the congregation. Good ideas that don't support the stated priorities are not pursued, so the congregation continues to minister out of the agreed-upon direction.

Every congregation operates with moments of brilliant insight related to mission and context. On a daily basis congregations experience a variety of temptations that threaten to detract them from their focus. These distractions take many forms including board and staff member turnover, budget crisis, building crisis, congregational conflict, and a lack of volunteers. Even wonderful new opportunities and creative new ideas can serve as strategic distractions for the church that isn't good at sustaining focus. Any new great idea or opportunity can take congregational leaders off track and away from clear focus on the fulfillment of its mission.

The goal of strategic leadership is alignment. The congregation is aligned when identity, vision, values, goals, and action plans fully support one another in a way that produces maximum organizational effectiveness. Alignment ensures that energies are not wasted and leaders are not burned out by getting sidetracked into issues that are not central to the strategic identity of the congregation.

What is the difference between strategic leadership and any other kind of leadership? Leadership in general is about the act of influencing others toward the pursuit of a common goal. I have encountered many clergy who possess good overall leadership skills, but they don't demonstrate particularly good strategic leadership. Although they are effective at creating vision, inspiring members of the congregation, and compelling people towards action, they are not good at sustaining focus on an overall strategy. They shift priorities continually, falling prey to what some refer to as a "flavor of the month" approach to leadership. Any great new idea captures the imagination of these leaders and they take the focus of their congregations with them as they pursue whatever new ideas spark their interest. Or they know how to inspire people toward action, but don't have any clue how to galvanize all of the different organizational parts of the congregation towards the same outcome, at the same time.

STRATEGIC LEADERSHIP IN THE LARGE CONGREGATION

All churches need good strategic leadership, regardless of the size. The large church is not unique in that regard. However, the larger a congregation becomes, the more central strategic leadership becomes to the success of the mission. In the smaller church one or two individuals in the organization can demonstrate good strategic leadership, and that might be enough to keep the entire congregation focused. The smaller congregation can simply call a congregational meeting, get everyone in the same room, and hammer out the decisions required to keep the church on track. In the multi-celled church, and even in some professional size churches, the staff team can gather around the same table and get clear about direction. Several key members of the staff team can attend a board meeting and effectively coordinate the joint activity of the board and staff team. However, once a church enters the strategic or matrix size categories, alignment is no longer a simple task. There are too many organizational building blocks that need to be factored into alignment. Even the most gifted individual leader can no longer power the church toward a specific focus. A leadership system that forms and executes strategy has to be carefully crafted.

The large church has the capacity to pursue with excellence almost anything that it decides it wants to do. Recently, leaders at Faith Presbyterian decided that they wanted to add a weekly Taizé service to their worship menu. It didn't take long for the staff team to identify two gifted musicians in the congregation who could provide the musical leadership needed for the service. Last year, Grand Valley United Methodist decided that it needed a more focused effort on young adult ministry to reach 25- to 35-year-olds. Within two months of having claimed this direction, the senior minister had identified three major donors who were willing to underwrite the salary and benefits of a new young adult ministry professional for a 24-month period, after which the program was expected to become self-funding. Neither of these efforts happened without considerable effort, but both initiatives illustrate the large church's capacity to pursue excellence.

The very capacity that enables the pursuit of excellence in the large congregation is also its strategic downfall. Although the large church has the capacity to pursue with excellence any given ministry, no large church has the capacity to pursue all things with excellence. No church is able be all things to all people. Every church has limited capacity and resources on some level. Choices have to be made about where time, energy, and resources will be directed. We may want to embrace a congregational culture that supports the passions of our individual leaders. We may want to encourage the ministry of the laity by supporting each good idea they present. In the large church, however, the pursuit of every good idea is a death knell for strategic alignment. The strategic leadership system of the church has to learn how to say no in service to a greater yes. The greater yes is the congregation's strategy for ministry.

In the book *Executing Your Strategy,* authors Mark Morgan, Raymond Levitt and William Malek, from the Stanford Advanced Project Management Program, call upon an old arcade game, "Whac-a-mole," to illustrate what often happens with leadership strategy in large organizations.[3] The game features six "moles" that pop up through holes in a game board directly in front of the player. Each player is given a club—"a mole whacker." As the game starts, moles pop up through the holes at random. The object of the game is to whack the mole on the head before it drops back into its hole and to make contact with as many moles as possible in a two-minute playing period. The best players hover ever so slightly over the playing board, ready to pounce upon whatever mole happens to emerge next. I love the analogy, and I am struck by how well it describes leadership in large congregations without strategic clarity.

In such a congregation, the latest and greatest idea always captures the energy of leaders, and their focus shifts rapidly from one emerging mole to the next, until all congregational leaders are fully engaged in an all-out game of Whac-a-mole. Staff members begin the game by laying out an incredible array of programs and ministries that are designed to encourage participation among members. Program participants add new holes to the Whac-a-mole board as they register their unmet needs. Governing board members watch the game play and add to the confusion of the game by suggesting yet more holes and moles that ought to be added to better position the congregation for ministry. When governing board members begin noticing that the staff team isn't keeping up with the number of moles popping up, the board members enter the game in the form of micromanagement. Board members become overly involved in directing the shape and pace of mole whacking. Whac-a-mole strategy looks exciting on the surface but quickly degenerates into exhaustion.

Another feature that adds to the complexity of strategic leadership in the large congregation is the fact that most large congregations are regional churches. They draw their membership base from wide geographic areas, encompassing multiple communities. In the large congregation it is not unusual to discover that a significant core of the participating body travels in excess of 20 or even 30 minutes, from different directions, to come to worship each week. Strategic leadership requires us to understand the demographics of the community we serve, and it requires that we articulate the ways in which our passions and strengths uniquely serve that demographic. A smaller congregation can typically look at the area that surrounds the physical plant of the church to formulate its strategic identity. Because the larger congregation draws from multiple communities, it often struggles when answering the question, "Who is our neighbor?" The large congregation discovers that the demographics of the community in which the church building is located may be different from the demographic of the communities that worshipers come from. And both of those communities may be different demographically from the communities that the congregation serves in mission. How does the large congregation decide to whom it will be neighbor?

Finally, a key strategic challenge for the large church lies in determining how to discern the vision, given the number of people who have a vested interest in naming it. Polity and theology inform the extent to which congregational members are expected to participate in the discernment of strategy. In more theologically conservative congregations, the discernment and articulation of strategic identity and direction rests firmly on the shoulders of the senior clergy leader. He (and it usually is a he) communes directly with God to discern and articulate the future direction of the congregation. The church's board of elders may have a strong voice in forming the vision, but the average person in the pew does not. In congregations with more liberal leanings or those that operate with a congregational polity, the governing board is charged with discerning the vision while honoring the collective voice of the congregation. The senior clergy leader is expected to catch the vision from the hearts and minds of congregants and articulate that vision back to membership.

It should be noted here that the life cycle of the congregation also determines how strongly the senior clergy relies on her own sense of the vision. In very young congregations, congregations experiencing crisis, or rapidly declining congregations, more authoritarian leadership styles are warranted. Effective leaders in these congregations rely more on the strength of their own vision than on discerning the vision of membership.

Most congregations operate somewhere in a middle ground, where the leader is expected to have a vision of her own but must also ensure that her vision is in sync with the vision in the hearts and minds of congregation members. Herein lays the challenge for the large congregation. How do leaders listen effectively to the voice of the congregation when those voices number in the hundreds and thousands?

This challenge is exacerbated by the fact that many people are drawn to the large congregation out of their desire to remain anonymous. Anonymous members bear expectations that are often tricky to negotiate. They may not want to be called out for leadership roles, but they do look to see if their own passions and interests are in alignment with the strategic identity and direction of the church. If those don't match their personal preferences and passion, these worshipers are likely to vote with their feet by taking their membership elsewhere. How do leaders get anonymous pew sitters to participate in the formation of strategic identity and direction? And should they?

Another challenge related to locating voice in the large congregation is to balance the voices of staff with the voices of lay leaders. Clearly, responsibility for forming the strategy rests firmly with the governing board of the congregation and the head of staff. However, the staff team is the operational arm of the congregation that brings the strategy to life through execution of the plan. If the staff team doesn't support the plan, it won't be properly executed. How does the large congregation involve the staff team in the articulation of strategy, without either letting the staff team become overly influential or ignoring the collective wisdom of staff members?

In the remainder of this chapter, I will lay out a model for thinking about and organizing strategic leadership in the large congregation. The model will consider strategy formation separately from strategy execution and will ultimately combine the two under the label of strategic engagement. Strategy formation and strategy execution each require four distinct leadership domains that must be coordinated. In total, this makes for eight leadership domains that must be simultaneously tended to produce effective strategic leadership in the large congregation.

STRATEGY FORMATION

There are four leadership domains in the formation of a congregation's strategy. These include:

- Form a mission identity
- Translate identity into strategy
- Articulate goals and measures
- Align structure and culture

These four domains must be completed and coordinated in order for a congregation to have a fully formed strategy. The formed strategy is no more than a coordinated set of intentions. The execution of strategy comes later. But without well-formed strategic intentions, the process of execution is meaningless. In the pages that follow we will explore each of these four leadership domains in greater detail. Figure 8.1 illustrates the interactive nature of the four tasks. A congregation with no strategy must begin with forming a mission identity. Once a mission identity has been articulated, leaders may proceed clockwise through the remaining tasks. However, at any point in time, leaders may stop to revisit a prior task, reshaping their prior work in light of new learning. A congregation that is executing an already formed strategy will cycle back through some of the formation steps as they encounter barriers to execution. In short, each to the four tasks influences and is influenced by the other tasks.

Figure 8.1 Strategy Formation

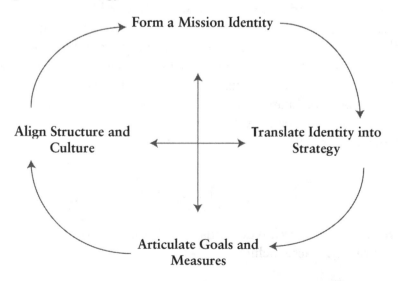

1. Form a Mission Identity

For many of us, the basic mission of our congregation is defined in the Scriptures we embrace and by the religious institutions that guide us. Every congregation on some level seeks to draw people into the congregation, transform them through their involvement with the congregation, and send them out to serve the larger world. In Christian congregations we often turn to passages like the Great Commission and the Great Commandment to articulate our reason for being. In any given context we may have very specific ways of carrying out the mission, but the core mission of congregations, in general, is a given.

In their book on strategic planning, *Holy Conversations*, Alban senior consultants Gil Rendle and Alice Mann make a distinction between the *axiomatic* mission of a congregation (the fundamental mission shared by all congregations of a given denominational system or religious body) and the *unique* mission of a congregation that is formed by its specific context, location, giftedness, and place in time.[4] A strategically led congregation understands both missions. Rendle and Mann propose three basic questions that can guide any congregation in more clearly articulating a mission unique to context:

- Who are we? (This is the identity question)
- Who is our neighbor? (This is the contextual question.)
- What is God calling us to do or become? (This is the purpose question.)[5]

In the illustration presented at the beginning of this chapter, we saw two congregations, one with strong strategic leadership and the other with weak strategic leadership. First Baptist is a good example of a congregation that had clarity about its axiomatic purpose but lacked clarity about its specific mission. The good people at First Baptist clearly understood that their job was to spread the Gospel, invite others to be transformed by the Gospel, and tend to the needs of a broken world. However, they had no idea how to articulate their unique mission. They didn't have any particular knowledge about their own distinctive identity (other than that they were a congregation of people who loved one another and felt like a family). They couldn't articulate anything particular about the unique nature of the community they served (other than that the community had stopped looking like them some time earlier), and they didn't have a clear urgency about purpose, beyond loving one another and whoever might show up on their doorstep. And because they didn't have clarity about their unique context, they ultimately lost their ability to serve the broader mission of the church. A congregation without clarity about how it will serve its context, employing its unique giftedness, rarely does an effective job of serving the larger mission of the church.

What is unique about forming a mission identity in the large congregation? In most respects claiming a mission identity is the same in any size congregation. A planning or self-study team is appointed by the governing board to lead the congregation in a process of self-reflection that may take anywhere from three to nine months to complete.

A congregation can typically address the "Who are we?" question through a careful compilation of internal data that charts membership, attendance, and giving trends. Available demographic data on the membership of the church can be augmented with a survey that asks members about their ministry preferences and their assessment of current ministries. Some surveys, such as the U.S. Congregational Life Survey,[6] provide a congregation with comparative data, so leaders can compare the responses of their congregation to other similarly sized or denominationally aligned congregations.

The "Who is our neighbor?" question can be addressed through community-leader interviews and demographic studies of targeted geographic areas around the church—ministry areas served by the church or from which membership is drawn.

The answer to the "What are we called to do or become?" question can be discerned through carefully crafted listening circles in which congregants are invited to reflect on the congregation's core values and dream about the next chapter of church life. More about each of these self-study and discernment techniques is available in *Holy Conversations*.

Smaller congregations may be able to pull significant parts of the whole system together to participate in each task of the strategy formation process. In the large congregation, the only task in which the congregation as a whole is invited to participate is this first one, the formation of mission identity. Every other stage of the process in the large church is managed by a sub-group of staff and lay leaders, on behalf of the larger congregation. Members of a large congregation might participate in this stage through a survey, an interview, or a listening session. Listening tools like the interview or focus group can target, at best, 10 to 20 percent of active members in the large congregation. But a well-orchestrated survey, given during worship or the Sunday school hour, can target 70 to 80 percent of active members. The communication effort required to solicit this level of involvement is significant.

The formation of mission identity is largely complete once a congregation is able to assemble a narrative document that provides answers to the first two strategic questions: *Who are we?* and *Who is our neighbor?* At this stage of work a congregation may have some sense of what God is calling the congregation to do or become, based on the hopes and dreams expressed by members and community leaders. However, more work needs to be done with those hopes and dreams before we can call them a strategy. At this stage they are still merely broad intentions. Typically, at the end of this stage of work I encourage my clients to prepare a short (one- to two-page) written synopsis of their learning to date.

2. Translate Identity into Strategy

Once the study team has completed its process of listening, study, and reflection, the congregation is ready to begin forming strategy. The three questions that form mission identity help to articulate the overall identity of the congregation, but the congregation's answers to those questions are not yet strategy.

The ideal forum in which to translate intention into strategy is the leadership retreat. I often encourage large congregations to assemble a group of at least 64 (eight tables of eight) leaders for a weekend. This large leadership community consists of all clergy and director-level staff, all current governing board members, and other key leaders whose buy-in to the strategy is important. In some congregations this may generate a leadership group of up to 125 leaders. The study team opens the retreat by sharing the findings that grew out of their listening and reflection process. Then the assembled leadership body works with an outside facilitator to create a strategy. For many years, congregations have been encouraged to form mission statements, vision statements, core values, strategies, and action plans as part of their formal strategic plans. I have found the formation of mission and vision statements a bland experience, at best. Study teams invest significant energy trying to articulate the mission of the congregation in ways that generally restate the axiomatic purpose of the congregation. Frankly, I just haven't found that mission and vision statements are all that helpful to the leadership life of the congregation. Instead, in the context of the leadership retreat, I encourage leaders to name the strengths of the congregation they seek to preserve moving forward, six to eight core values, and two to four strategic priorities for the next few years. Let's look at each of these in greater depth.

The strengths of the congregation are specific areas of ministry or areas of leadership that are hallmark features of the church. These are the things that are so important to membership and so strongly associated with the congregation's identity that their essence must be preserved moving forward, regardless of changes anticipated. Examples include:

- Intellectually engaging sermons and worship services.
- Nurturing the well-being and spiritual development of our children through quality worship, music, and education venues targeted at their specific needs.
- A formal style of Sunday morning worship, with high quality music, surroundings, and a traditional order of service.
- Adequate, appropriate physical space to accommodate our programs and services, with support systems—such as food

and childcare—necessary to support those activities and encourage congregational involvement.
* Clergy staff who are regarded as leaders in the community and in the denomination.

Articulating a list of strengths to preserve helps leaders in two ways. First, it encourages leaders and members to be absolutely clear about what is most important, that which must never be compromised. Second, it helps leaders and members relax as they live into a change process by assuring everyone that the critical core will be maintained as change is introduced.

The core values of a congregation are those guiding principles and beliefs that shape the church. A congregation may operate with an entire universe of values, but some of them are so primary, so important, that throughout changes in internal membership and the external community they are still the core values. Core values might include headings like these: excellence in worship, beauty in the arts, caring for one another, the value of every voice, speaking truth to power, the importance of childhood, promoting social justice, openness to theological diversity, etc. Core values are *not* descriptions of the ministry or work a congregation does. They are principles that the congregation holds dear. Consider these more fully defined examples:

Welcome/Openness/Diversity
We believe that God is love, and that in the name of a loving God we are called to extend welcome to all God's children, our brothers and sisters. As we learn to get beyond barriers such as race, class, and sexual orientation, we become a community more truly reflective of the God who calls us together.

Progressive Theology
We believe that our theological expression must continually grow and change to encompass new understandings of God's leading in the world. With Scripture and tradition as our guide, we welcome the challenge that faces each generation to formulate a theology that will allow timeless truth to be heard afresh and lived anew.

Worship Excellence
Through worship we seek to engage the whole person—heart and soul, strength and mind—in giving expression to our love for God. We cherish preaching that is challenging and inspiring, and music that is beautiful and uplifting. Worship helps us reflect on our lives, renew our commitment, and discover the power and presence of God in our lives.

When a congregation has clarity about its core values, leaders are better equipped to make decisions on the congregation's behalf. Whenever multiple options for moving forward exist, leaders can consider these core values before deciding what to do.

Finally, the strategic priorities of a congregation are those few initiatives that the congregation will pursue over the next three to five years as it tries to live more fully into its mission identity. The strategic priorities represent those critical new areas of emphasis that will raise existing programming to new levels of excellence, stretch members in new ways, or introduce previously unexplored areas of ministry that are consistent with the mission identity. The strategic priorities typically emerge from the hopes and dreams of the congregation, particularly where they intersect with identified needs of our neighbors.

Consider the following strategic initiatives claimed by the leaders of Faith Lutheran Church at a recent leadership retreat. Leaders expect these initiatives to consume much of the congregation's resources and energy over the next five years. The initiatives have to do with deepening the congregation's spirituality and forming stronger communities through intergenerational cohorts, specifically through the use of small groups. Here's how leaders chose to define these two broad-based initiatives. Notice that at this stage of strategy formation, the new priorities are written very generally. Each strategic initiative is a broad statement of intention followed by statements that describe what the congregation will look like if the initiative is successfully accomplished. Leaders are not yet trying to write goal statements or name the specific venues that will be used to bring about these outcomes.

Living in the Spirit

We are a faith community that celebrates and explores our common bond in Christ and our passion for living in the Spirit. We invite the community to join us as we become more intentional about spiritual renewal and spiritual growth. We seek God's will in our decisions as individuals and as a church. We will be:

- A church known for spiritual development that includes both theological learning and the natural extension of this learning to our thoughts and deeds;
- Christians who practice their spiritual beliefs, reflecting those beliefs in every aspect of their lives, including a willingness to invest time, talent, and resources;
- Individuals who respect and encourage Christ-centered dialogue on theological issues and beliefs;
- People known for welcoming all in spiritual communion and for discipleship that helps all to connect to the Holy Spirit;
- Christians engaged in thoughtful decision making that seeks God's will (spiritual discernment).

Living in Community

Faith Lutheran will develop a small group ministry to tend to the faith development, care, and support of its membership. Small groups will organize according to life stages, including but not limited to children, youth, young families, older members, and senior citizens.

As we achieve this goal, there will be:

- Strengthened youth ministries (extending to college and young singles);
- Increased emphasis on and delivery of services for young families;
- Services for senior citizens;
- A place where old and new members have a sense of belonging and a sense of mission through involvement in groups, committees, and ministries that have meaning to them.

3. Articulate Goals and Measures

By the conclusion of the leadership retreat, leaders are clear about the broad strokes of the congregation's strategic identity. They know what core values they will honor in their decision making, what congregational strengths they must seek to preserve, and what the key strategic growth priorities of the congregation will be in its next chapter. What they don't yet know are the specific ways in which those priorities will be pursued.

Typically, at this stage in the strategy formation process, some new players need to be recruited. Leaders who may not have been on the planning team or governing board may need to be invited in. For example, Faith Lutheran realized that if they were going to pursue young adult and senior adult ministry more seriously, then they needed to invite some leaders into the planning process who had been involved in prior efforts in those ministry areas. Those leaders had not been involved in planning efforts to date, but their voices were critical for moving forward. To that end, the congregation formed two ad hoc committees to further study and shape the strategic initiatives claimed at the retreat. Each committee was made up of five to seven members (the outer threshold limit of a good decision-making group) and contained relevant staff and lay leaders with interest in and passion for the claimed strategic initiative. Each committee included at least one member from the mission identity study team and at least one staff member; at least half of the team was made up of leaders who had attended the strategy retreat. Each committee was charged with creating a more specific plan for the strategic initiative that had been assigned them. They were asked to look at the current state of the church, with regard to the new initiative, and then gauge the distance to be closed between the current state and the desired future state. Their task would be complete once they submitted a finished set of goals, action plans, and measures for the pursuit of that strategic initiative.

Once the specific action plans are assembled, the congregation has a full set of documents that make up a strategic plan, which they are ready to bring to the governing body of the congregation for approval. The approved document should include:

- Congregational core value statements;
- Congregational strengths to preserve;
- Two to three key strategic initiatives;
- A set of goal statements, action plans, and measures for each strategic initiative.

Many congregations believe that once the governing board of the congregation has approved the strategic planning document, they have completed the process of strategy formation, but one critical leadership task remains.

4. Align Structure and Culture

The goals and action plans of newly claimed strategic initiatives often present the congregation with work to be done that is not supported by the existing congregational structure and culture. When a congregation attempts to introduce new ways of doing things into an infrastructure that can't support it, the congregation sets itself up for failure. New wine calls for new wineskins.

At Faith Lutheran, leaders quickly realized two important structural problems that would prevent the congregation from realizing the dreams expressed in their new strategic initiatives. The first realization was that plans called for a great deal of orchestrated communication across various ministry areas, but no one on the staff team had overall ownership of the communication function. A new full-time position, director of communication, was created to address the need.

The second realization had to do with the design of the committee structure of the congregation. The new initiatives were going to increase the focus on generational cohorts within the congregation and require better coordination of the ministries across cohorts. Leaders realized that the present structure of the church, with separate committees attending to each generational cohort's need, was quickly going to lead to a disjointed ministry effort. A new adult discipleship team was formed to consolidate and better coordinate the ministry effort across cohorts and to house the oversight of small groups. This team replaced all previous teams for women's ministry, men's ministry, singles ministry, and senior adult ministry. The new ministry team was made up of seven individuals. The reorganization resulted in four fewer committees and freed up fifteen people who had been serving on these committees to participate more actively in hands-on ministry.

Once the strategic planning document has been adopted by the governing body of the congregation and the structures of the church have been aligned to support the initiatives named in that document, we can say that the congregation has a fully formed strategy, ready for execution. Of course, without execution, the formation of strategy is a worthless endeavor.

STRATEGY EXECUTION

I have worked with countless large congregations who have spent an intense year focused on strategy formation, only to have leaders set the plan on the shelf and watch it die. Leaders sometimes act as if the intention to be more strategic is enough. We operate as if leadership's deciding what its priorities ought to be will ensure that those strategies take hold in the life of a congregation. Nothing could be further from the truth. Any large church leader will tell you that the continual distractions of managing the large congregation unceasingly pull leadership energy away from its strategic focus. Unless something or someone keeps calling leaders back to their strategic focus, the strategy of the congregation will remain an unrealized dream. A congregation that wants to carry out the strategy that leaders have worked so hard to name must tend to four additional leadership domains. Strategy execution requires that leaders:

1. Provide board oversight
2. Transfer management responsibility to the staff
3. Allocate resources according to plan
4. Monitor and adapt

Figure 8.2 Strategy Execution

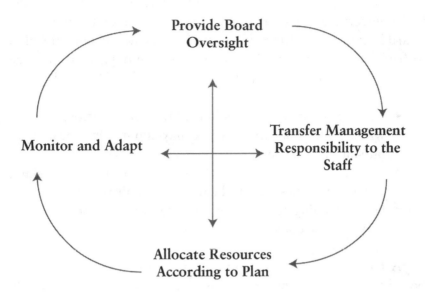

1. Provide Board Oversight

The governing board of the church is the only body within the church that can realistically accept oversight responsibility for the congregation's strategy. The board has the clearest authority to make decisions and allocate assets on behalf of the congregation. It can maintain the clearest focus on the future and the big picture, without getting dragged into the day-to-day minutia of managing church life.

Many large congregations act as if the staff team is the key strategic body of the congregation. They confuse the managerial work of the staff team with the duties of oversight. The staff team cannot effectively function as the oversight body of the church, however. A formal strategic plan details how the congregation expects to move from current circumstance to a preferred state. The process requires a focus on both the present reality and the preferred future. A staff team is designed to focus on the managerial here and now of a congregation. The board is better suited to keep its eye on the future and to remind church leaders of the transitions that need to take place to live into that preferred future.

Accepting oversight responsibility does *not* mean that the board undertakes the execution of the plan. In fact, the moment a board begins to function as if it is responsible for bringing the plan to fruition, the board has lost the perspective required to provide oversight. Accepting responsibility for oversight, the board:

- names the outcomes on behalf of the congregation;
- writes policy that defines what may and may not be done in pursuit of those outcomes;
- invites accountability into the leadership system by asking provocative questions and calling for evaluation;
- hosts planning forums (retreats) to evaluates progress and make course corrections to the strategy.

A more thorough discussion about the oversight role of the board is found in chapter 6 of this book, which deals specifically with board function and governance processes.

2. Transfer Management Responsibility to Staff

As the managerial body of the church, the staff team puts flesh and bones on strategic intent. Staff members engage laity in the creative design and delivery of worship, service, and programming needed to fulfill the strategic plan. Individual staff members do not reinvent the strategy of the congregation. Rather they execute ministries in accord with the strategy that congregational leaders have defined.

Strategic alignment in the large church is best served by a system of performance management. A good system of performance management entails well-defined staff roles. Every staff member should be clear about three components of their individual roles:

- The essential functions of the position (the duties and tasks she is expected to fulfill);
- The core competencies required for their position (the behaviors, skills, and abilities that the person in the role is expected to demonstrate);

- The performance goals for the year (specific expectations about how each member of the staff team is expected to help bring the strategic plan to fruition in the current year).

Furthermore, staff team meetings should be designed with a focus on the strategic priorities of the congregation. The overall performance management of the staff team and its roles in strategic leadership is further discussed in chapter 5 of this book and in *When Moses Meets Aaron,* by Rendle and Beaumont.

3. Allocate Resources According to Plan

A common reason strategic plans fail is that they are never fully owned in the moment when the resources of the congregation are allocated, and at levels beyond the governing board. The board and the executive staff team steep themselves in the nuances of the plan, but two levels down in the organizational structure of the church . . . no one has heard about it.

The most obvious place where strategic priorities need to be clear is in the annual budgeting process. A reasonable person ought to be able to review a church operating budget and understand something about its strategic priorities as a congregation. Furthermore, the capital campaign and fundraising plans of the congregation need to address the pieces of strategy that require a significant infusion of funding—new space requirements, new staff positions, technology upgrades, and so forth. The need to align resources with strategy does not end at the executive level.

When I am called into churches to conduct staffing assessments, I often find myself in interviews with staff members who are two or three reporting levels below the senior clergy person. I like to ask them to tell me something about the congregation's strategic plan and what it has to do with them. I am appalled at the number of times that they've never heard of the strategic plan and aren't really sure if the congregation has one. Even those who are familiar with the plan can rarely articulate what, if anything, it has to do with them and their work.

On a day-to-day basis a congregation lives out its strategic plan according to how the most mundane of decisions are made.

How should I spend my time today? What values should inform the decisions I make today? What priorities should shape how I allocate the resources that are mine to manage? Every member of the staff team and every committee or task force participant should have a working knowledge of the congregation's strategy. They should be able to articulate how the strategy is shaping their decision making.

The receptionist at the front desk who also schedules the use of meeting space in the church is a key strategic player. Does he know how the strategy of the church informs the decisions he makes about room assignments? Most custodians in congregations have to make daily choices regarding room setups and facility care. Do they understand the strategy of the church and what their priorities ought to be in any given moment?

Staff members should be grounded in the strategic priorities of the congregation in a variety of ways. Their ongoing conversations with a supervisor should continually draw them back to the strategic priorities of the congregation. The agenda of the staff meetings should also provide a weekly touchstone to the missional identity of the congregation.

Committee members should also be reminded of their part in the strategy of the congregation. The items placed on a meeting agenda should reflect the strategic initiatives of the church. A strategic approach to preaching should remind even the most anonymous of church members that the church has a strategy and that they bear responsibility for the execution of that strategy.

4. Monitor and Adapt

This final step in the execution of strategy is perhaps the biggest stumbling block for congregations. Congregations are allergic to evaluation. Sarah Drummond has written a marvelous text on the practice of planning and evaluation, *Holy Clarity*. Drummond opens the book with this simple statement, "Leadership and evaluation are not separate disciplines. Evaluative activities are part of the work of a leader, and some of the best practices of evaluation mirror the qualities that make a leader effective."[7]

The strategic alignment of a congregation requires evaluation at multiple levels. The board needs to evaluate the leadership of the senior clergy leader. The board also needs to evaluate its own performance and the congregation's performance against its strategic plan. The board should also invite an annual review of each strategic ministry area of the church. This should be conducted *with* (not on behalf of) the staff member who leads that area of ministry. For example, according to a predetermined schedule, the minister of music may be called into the February meeting of the board to reflect on the music ministry of the church, to talk about strategic challenges and opportunities, and to make decisions with the board about new strategic directions. The questions that will be discussed and the format of the ministry evaluation should be laid out in advance of the meeting. The leaders of other strategic ministry areas are called in other designated months to evaluate their ministries. Note that this evaluation is not a performance evaluation of the staff member. It is an evaluation of an area of ministry. An excellent resource that provides formats for evaluating ministry is Jill Hudson's book *Evaluating Ministry: Principles and Processes for Clergy and Congregations*.[8]

Each member of the staff team should receive an annual performance evaluation of her individual work, and that evaluation should be delivered by the staff person's direct supervisor—not by the board or a committee with whom the individual works. Staff evaluations should provide feedback about the staff member's performance in three areas: the essential functions of the role, the core competencies of the role, and their annual performance goals. See *When Moses Meets Aaron: Staffing and Supervision in the Large Congregation* for a more complete explanation of the staff performance evaluation process.[9]

The large church never met a program that it didn't like. We love starting up programs, and we avoid shutting them down like we avoid the H1N1 virus. There is always someone, somewhere, who is passionate about even the most obscure and poorly supported programs in our congregations. We seek not to offend. But if a congregation is going to be strategically aligned, leaders must evaluate individual programs to determine their effectiveness and to evaluate whether they are still in keeping with the congregation's mission. Individual programs should be evaluated in the appropriate board or committee that provides oversight to that ministry. Laity and staff members who lead the ministry should be included in the evaluation conversation. Drummond's book is an outstanding resource for approaching program evaluation. So is Kathleen Cahalan's book *Projects that Matter: Successful Planning and Evaluation for Religious Organizations*. Cahalan reminds us that projects and programs are always created to address a condition or set of conditions. The conditions that give birth to a program are unique, and we need to regularly reevaluate both the context and the intervention (program) to determine whether our response is still appropriate.[10]

Evaluation is not really a strategic activity unless we also adapt the strategy of the congregation based upon the results of our evaluation. The core values, congregational strengths, and strategic initiatives of a congregation ought to be fairly stable elements of a congregation's strategic identity. It's rare that a congregation would adapt one of these elements of strategy in response to a program or ministry area evaluation. However, the goals, action plans, and metrics that make up the remainder of a church's strategy are much more fluid elements of design, and the governing board of the church should feel free to modify them in response to information gleaned during evaluation. For example, Faith Lutheran discovered at the end of year one of its plan that the curriculum it planned to design for small groups already existed in a form that is useable in its context. Purchasing the curriculum will be more cost effective than having a staff member write it. Faith decided to change its action plans to include this purchase.

Every year that a plan is in effect, the board should be issuing an updated strategic plan that incorporates all of the congregation's progress to date and any revisions to goals and action plans that arise in response to the congregation's evaluation.

STRATEGIC ENGAGEMENT: PUTTING IT ALL TOGETHER

Strategic engagement is what happens when strategy formation and strategy execution intersect. Many large congregations approach strategic planning like the deployment of an airplane. They invest considerable effort in strategy formation, which is the organizational equivalent of a plane taking off. Takeoff uses a lot of fuel. It is the segment of the journey that contains the most risk and may be the most unpleasant for passengers. The plane doesn't cover many horizontal miles during takeoff, because it's focusing all of its energy on getting to cruising altitude.

The forward momentum of the congregation often feels like it is slowed to a halt during strategy formation. Leadership energy goes into planning, not ministry. Once the congregation begins to execute the plan, leaders hit the equivalent of cruising altitude, at least for a brief period of time. The congregation makes progress on some of its goals and initiatives. If leadership changes, if energies wane, or if the congregation loses its focus, it isn't long before leaders discover that the congregation has glided back toward the ground. Several years down the road we notice that the congregation is once again motionless, and some new leader asks, "Shouldn't we be doing some self-study and planning, or something?" Preparation for takeoff begins all over again.

Effective strategic engagement is a fluid and ongoing process. The congregation that demonstrates good strategic engagement doesn't waste the energy invested in takeoff. Leaders are continually engaged in evaluation, self-reflection, and adaptation, keeping the organization at cruising altitude indefinitely. The learning that occurs during evaluation is used to reshape vision identity, claim new strategies, articulate new priorities ,and make ongoing adjustments to internal structure, all the while that the congregation is in motion. The strategic large church refuels in the air, not back on the ground.

Figure 8.3 Strategic Engagement

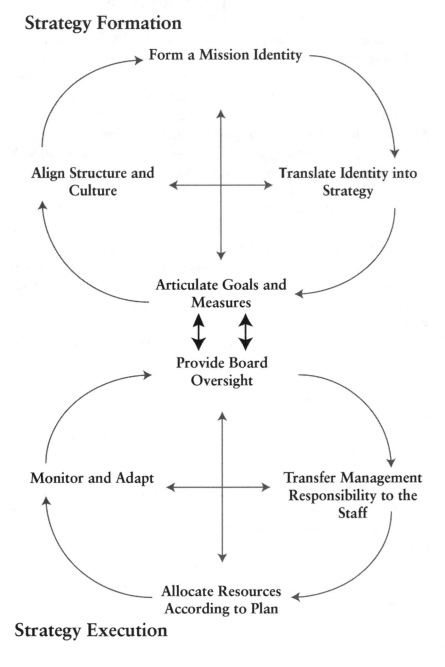

Strategy Formation

Form a Mission Identity

Align Structure and Culture

Translate Identity into Strategy

Articulate Goals and Measures

Provide Board Oversight

Monitor and Adapt

Transfer Management Responsibility to the Staff

Allocate Resources According to Plan

Strategy Execution

QUESTIONS FOR INDIVIDUAL OR GROUP REFLECTION

1. Strategic leadership is the ability to think, act, and influence in ways that promote sustainable focus on the congregation's unique mission. Do you think of yourself as an effective strategic leader? Which part of the strategic leadership equation is most challenging for you: thinking, acting, or influencing?

2. Can you articulate the vision identity of your congregation in a simple paragraph (or verbally in 30 seconds)? If so, do you address all three of the basic strategy questions: Who are we? Who is our neighbor? What is God calling us to do or become? If your congregation does not have a clear strategic identity, what would it take to develop one?

3. This chapter makes a distinction between strategy formation and strategy execution, referring to the intersection of the two as strategic engagement. How effective is your congregation at strategic engagement? Historically, have your leaders been more focused on strategy formation or execution? What has prevented you from doing a better job with strategic engagement?

GROUP EXERCISE: STRATEGIC LEADERSHIP EVALUATION

This chapter discussed eight basic domains involved in good strategic leadership. On the pages that follow you will be invited to reflect upon and evaluate your congregation's performance in each of those domains. Have each member of your group complete the evaluation individually. Participants should be instructed to read each statement and assign a score from 1 to 5, evaluating the performance of the congregation over the past 12-month period, against the standard that is described by the statement. The ratings associated with each number (1 to 5) are described at the top of every page.

1. After a score has been assigned to each individual statement, invite participants to assign an average score to each section. There is no need to pull out calculators and engage in complicated mathematical averaging. Simply invite them to eyeball their responses and assign a score to the category based upon their overall impression.

2. When each individual has completed the scoring, divide the larger group into small groups of six to eight individuals. Invite each small group to come to consensus on a group score for every category. Discourage the groups from averaging their scores in order to arrive at consensus. Instead invite them to reflect upon the highest and lowest individual responses they assigned in each category and why they settled upon their individual score for the category. Encourage the group to reach consensus through dialogue.

3. When all of the small groups have completed their assessments, invite a representative of each small group to enter their group scores for each category onto the scoring matrix on page 234. (Note: The large group facilitator may want to reproduce this chart on a wall chart, so everyone can view the scores as they are entered.)

To what extent does each of the following statements describe leadership practices in your congregation? Rank each statement on a scale of 1 to 5.

1 = Not at all or never
2 = Not much or rarely
3 = Somewhat or occasionally
4 = Mostly or usually
5 = Completely or always

1. Form a Mission Identity

1. Our leaders have a shared understanding about the basic reason the congregation exists. ___
2. Our leaders can articulate what is unique about our congregation—what sets us apart from other congregations in our geographic area and other congregations in our denominational system. ___
3. Our leaders know whom we are here to serve. ___
4. Our leaders understand the neighborhood surrounding our congregation. ___
5. Our leaders can articulate a relationship with and mission to our immediate neighbors. ___

Average Score: ___

2. Translate Identity into Strategy

1. Our leaders are in consensus about the strengths of our congregation that need to be preserved moving forward. ___
2. We have a clearly defined set of core values that accurately state our core principles and beliefs. ___
3. Our leaders are clear about three to five strategic priorities of this chapter in congregational life. ___

Average Score: ___

To what extent does each of the following statements describe leadership practices in your congregation? Rank each statement on a scale of 1 to 5.

1 = Not at all or never
2 = Not much or rarely
3 = Somewhat or occasionally
4 = Mostly or usually
5 = Completely or always

3. Articulate Priorities, Goals and Measures

1. Our leaders have a written plan that describes the goals and action plans we are trying to accomplish in the next one, three, and five years? ___
2. Leaders have agreed-upon measures of performance that allow us to evaluate our progress against goals. ___
3. The measures that have been set to evaluate our progress against goals are appropriate measures of those goals. ___
4. Leaders regularly review our long-term goals and adjust our short-term plans to align with our long-term goals. ___
5. The congregation's priorities, goals, and measures are well communicated to all who need to know. ___
6. Leaders receive timely and accurate information that helps them evaluate where we stand in supporting our priorities and goals. ___

Average Score: ___

To what extent does each of the following statements describe leadership practices in your congregation? Rank each statement on a scale of 1 to 5.

1 = Not at all or never
2 = Not much or rarely
3 = Somewhat or occasionally
4 = Mostly or usually
5 = Completely or always

4. Align Structure and Culture

1. The design and size of our staff team is appropriate to accomplish our articulated priorities and goals. ___
2. The design and size of our governing board is appropriate for accomplishing our articulated priorities and goals. ___
3. We have an appropriate committee and team structure in place to accomplish our priorities and goals. ___
4. Our governance process lends itself to effective decision making and communication. ___
5. The board and committee structure of the church is flexible and adaptable, as needed to accommodate new ways of doing ministry. ___
6. The congregation has demonstrated the ability to change in meaningful ways. ___
7. There is a sense of excitement and anticipation among members about our church's future. ___
8. Members are appropriately informed about what the board, committees, ministry teams, and staff team of the congregation are doing. ___
9. The artifacts of our culture (processes, rituals, stories, physical environment) are consistent with and support our strategy. ___

Average Score: ___

To what extent does each of the following statements describe leadership practices in your congregation? Rank each statement on a scale of 1 to 5.

1 = Not at all or never
2 = Not much or rarely
3 = Somewhat or occasionally
4 = Mostly or usually
5 = Completely or always

5. Provide Board Oversight

1. The board understands itself as being owned by the mission of the congregation, not by congregation members. ___
2. Board members commit adequate time, energy, and attention to the strategic leadership of the congregation. ___
3. Board members are prepared for meetings and regularly attend and participate. ___
4. Board members comply with the congregation's foundational documents (constitution, bylaws, canons, and denominational rulebooks). ___
5. The board operates with a comprehensive set of policies (authorized written statements), so board time is not wrapped up in routine decision making. ___
6. The board sets its agenda to avoid excessive time spent receiving reports. ___
7. The board delegates the day-to-day management of the church to the staff team and avoids micromanagement. ___
8. The board focuses the majority of its meeting time on the strategic work of the congregation. ___
9. The board fulfills its duty of care to ensure that the congregation's human and material resources are used for the benefit of its mission. ___
10. The board empowers a small subset of board members (an executive team) to make decisions between meetings. ___

Average Score: ___

To what extent does each of the following statements describe leadership practices in your congregation? Rank each statement on a scale of 1 to 5.

1 = Not at all or never
2 = Not much or rarely
3 = Somewhat or occasionally
4 = Mostly or usually
5 = Completely or always

6. Transfer Management Responsibility to the Staff

1. The staff team understands itself as being owned by the mission of the congregation and not by the congregants or board members. ___
2. Each staff member operates with a well-defined role as outlined in a regularly updated job description. ___
3. Each staff member operates with a set of clearly defined goals that align the work of the individual staff member with the missional priorities of the congregation. ___
4. Each staff member has one supervisor who helps to prioritize the staff member's work and provides ongoing feedback. ___
5. Every employee participates in a comprehensive annual performance appraisal during which goals for the prior year are reviewed and goals for the coming year are established. ___
6. Each member of the staff team engages in an appropriately configured weekly staff meeting where strategy is emphasized and joint work is negotiated. ___
7. The staff team is organized into meaningful sub-teams that allow people with similar functional roles to work effectively together. ___
8. Sub-units of the staff team appropriately collaborate with other sub-units of the team. ___
9. Supervisors have an adequate span of control (a reasonable number of direct reports), which allows them to spend sufficient supervision time with each employee. ___

10. A small subset of senior staff persons operates as an executive team to align the overall work of the team and triage staff issues, so they are directed to the appropriate part of the team. (This is only appropriate for the strategic and matrix sized congregation.) ___

Average Score: ___

7. Allocate Resources According to Plan

1. An annual operating budget is proposed by the staff team and approved by the governing board ___
2. The annual operating budget is structured to support the strategic priorities of the congregation. ___
3. Staff, lay leaders, and congregational members support decisions made in the budgeting process, once those decision have been approved by the governing board. ___
4. The budgeting process invites leaders to evaluate proposed activities, saying yes to those activities that are in alignment with strategy, and saying no to those activities that are not. ___
5. Private agendas are kept out of the budgeting process. ___

Average Score: ___

To what extent does each of the following statements describe leadership practices in your congregation? Rank each statement on a scale of 1 to 5.

1 = Not at all or never
2 = Not much or rarely
3 = Somewhat or occasionally
4 = Mostly or usually
5 = Completely or always

8. Monitor and Adapt

1. Our information systems provide us with appropriate information to track progress in most program and ministry areas.
2. Ongoing programs and ministries of the congregation are evaluated on a regular cycle of review.
3. Programs and ministries that are no longer in alignment with the missional priorities of the congregation are retired.
4. Programs and ministries that are no longer effective are re-purposed or retired.
5. The congregation manages a portfolio of programs and ministries that is consistent with its strategy.
6. The congregation maintains a portfolio of programs and ministries that can be well managed within the capacity of our resources.
7. Leaders annually update our goals and priorities, based upon actual results attained.
8. Leaders annually update our goals and priorities to reflect what is happening in our internal and external environment.

Average Score: ___

Scoring Matrix

To be used in a group context to collect and reflect on small group scores. Enter the average scores for each group in the matrix below.

Leadership Domain	Group 1	Group 2	Group 3	Group 4
Form a Mission Identity				
Translate Identity into Strategy				
Articulate Goals and Measures				
Align Structure and Culture				
Provide Board Oversight				
Transfer Mgt. Responsibility to Staff				
Allocate Resources According to Plan				
Monitor and Adapt				

Invite the larger group to reflect on the collective results posted on the wall chart.

a. In which domain(s) of strategic engagement do we demonstrate the greatest strength?

b. Where do we appear to be weakest or most inconsistent?

c. Where are we most in agreement about our evaluations?

d. Where do we seem to see things most differently? What accounts for that difference?

e. Where might we begin to strengthen our strategic engagement?

Ending with a Beginning in Mind

Some of you may have read this book from beginning to end in a linear fashion. Others of you may have dipped in and out of chapters, focusing on those leadership systems where you are experiencing the greatest pain or sense of disorientation. Whatever your approach, my hope is that you have a greater sense of clarity about your focus, about what needs to change first in your congregation to get your systems rightsized. If that is not the case and you feel a sense of panic about all of the work your congregation needs to do to better align its leadership system, don't despair. All is not lost. Even small course corrections in the right direction can make a big change in the leadership effectiveness of a congregation. Rather than yielding to a sense of feeling overwhelmed, simply ask, "What is one good step that I could take to make a difference in the right direction?" And then, pursue that step.

I have taken you through an understanding of how size influences five key leadership systems in the large church: clergy roles, staff team function and design, governance and board structure, acculturation and the assimilation of laity, and the formation and execution of strategy. I have yet to encounter a congregation that has all five leadership systems perfectly aligned to appropriately serve its size. Most congregations have significant work to do in one or more (sometimes, all five) of the leadership systems described. The challenge is not to try to figure out an overall game plan for perfectly rightsizing all of your leadership systems. That will never happen. Just as you manage to align the staff team and board structure, something will change in your environment that pushes another leadership system out of alignment. The challenge is in trying to figure out where to begin.

In an ideal world the best place to begin is with strategy. *If* a congregation has a healthy board structure that will allow it to do good planning, and *if* the congregation has enough time and space to engage in good planning, begin with a strategic plan. Once the congregation's mission and strategy have been clearly articulated, then leaders can more effectively define the role of the clergy, the design of the staff team and board structure, the role of the laity, and so forth.

However, most congregation leaders don't minister in an ideal world. Perhaps your board is functioning so poorly that leaders can't possible provide effective oversight to a good strategic planning process. Or perhaps the design of your staff team is so broken that staff cannot come up for air to get perspective on strategy and their role in it. Perhaps a budget crisis is forcing you to downsize your staff team, and you need to make some decisions about staffing structure now, without the benefit of a good strategy. Maybe the role of laity is so misunderstood in your congregation that getting clarity on the decision-making role of lay leaders is critical, before you can create a good strategic plan.

Here is the bottom line. When picking a place to begin, you need to focus on the leadership system that is causing the greatest pain for the largest number of people. That is often the best place to gain leverage that will positively benefit the other systems. If you are experiencing massive disorientation or pain around several leadership systems at the same time, then focus on the one that your leadership body seems to care most about. If the leadership energies of your congregation are most piqued by conversations about governance and board structure, begin there. If there is significant dissatisfaction with the role of laity in the church, begin with that system. If all else fails, go with your own intuition and follow your own energies.

No leadership system stands alone. A congregation is a living and breathing organism, and each of the four systems outlined in this book is so intertwined with the other four that you can't possibly begin work on one without the other five experiencing some repercussions. Be prepared for the ramifications of this. Communicate the changes that are happening in one area, so the other four leadership systems understand why they are experiencing shifts and pinch points in their work as well.

Large congregations are dynamic and intriguing institutions to lead. If you are a leader in a large congregation, then you face daily opportunities that are challenging, fun, growth-producing, exciting—and frustrating. My prayer for you is that most days will be about the fun, excitement, growth, and challenge, and that your days of frustration will be minimal. On those days when the frustration outweighs the fun, I pray that you will remember how blessed you are to be entrusted with the ministry of a large congregation. You touch an extraordinary number of lives by virtue of your leadership. May you be blessed on the journey.

NOTES

Part 1: Size Does Matter

Chapter 1: Why Size Matters: The Large Church in Context

1. Scott Thumma and Dave Travis *Beyond Megachurch Myths: What We Can Learn From America's Largest Churches* (San Francisco: John Wiley & Sons, 2007), 7.
2. Ibid., 9.
3. Mark Chaves, "The National Congregations Study: American Congregations at the Beginning of the 21st Century," 2006-2007, accessed at http://www.soc.duke.edu/natcong, 2–3.
4. Ibid., 2–3.
5. Ibid., 3.
6. Hartford Institute for Religion Research, http://hirr.hartsem.edu/research/fastfacts/fast_facts.html#growlose
7. Lyle E. Schaller, *The Very Large Church: New Rules for Leaders* (Nashville: Abingdon Press, 2000), 31–32.
8. Ibid., 36.
9. Mark Chaves, "The National Congregations Study," 7–8.
10. Robert D. Putnam, *Bowling Alone: The Collapse and Revival of American Community* (New York: Simon and Schuster, 2000), 18–19.
11. Ibid., 65–79.
12. Mark Chaves, "The National Congregations Study," 6–7.
13. Eddie Gibbs, *Churchmorph: How Megatrends are Reshaping Christian Communities* (Grand Rapids: Baker Academic, 2009), 21–24.

Chapter 2: How Size Changes Things

1. R. Dunbar (1993). "Coevolution of neocortex size, group size and language in humans," *Behavioral & Brain Sciences,* 16(4): 681–735.

2. Theodore W. Johnson, "Current Thinking on Size Transitions," *Size Transitions in Congregations*, Beth Ann Gaede, editor (Herndon, VA: Alban Institute, 1989), 3–29.
3. "How to Design Small Decision Making Groups," http://www.intuitor.com/statistics/SmallGroups.html.

Chapter 3: Living Large: Exploring Large Church Size Categories

1. Eric Carle, *A House for Hermit Crab* (New York: Simon and Schuster Publishing, 1987).
2. These are the three questions posed by Gil Rendle and Alice Mann in *Holy Conversations* (Herndon, VA: Alban Institute, 2003), that constitute the essence of a congregation's strategic identity.
3. The metaphor of the spider and the starfish have been adapted from Ori Brafman and Rod A. Beckstrom, *The Starfish and the Spider: The Unstoppable Power of Leaderless Organizations* (London: Penguin Books, 2006).
4. Ibid., 35.

Part 2: Leadership Systems in Motion

Chapter 4: Clergy Leadership Roles

1. Louis B. Weeks, *All For God's Glory: Redeeming Church Scutwork* (Herndon, VA: The Alban Institute, 2008), 6.
2. Taken from a whitepaper, "Stewardship and Fundraising as Ministry" by David Ruhe, Senior Minister of Plymouth Congregational UCC, Des Moines, October 4, 2010.
3. The section of the chapter that addresses the role of associate clergy originally appeared in the Fall 2009 issue of *Congregations* magazine, under the title "Specialist or Generalist? The Associate Pastor Role in the Large Church."
4. Gil Rendle and Susan Beaumont, When Moses Meets Aaron: Staffing and Supervision in Large Congregations (Herndon, VA: The Alban Institute, 2007) 10.
5. For more information on how to create a performance management system for the staff, the reader is referred to Part 2 of When Moses Meets Aaron by Rendle and Beaumont.
6. Colleen Pepper, "Inside the World of Executive Pastors: Leadership Network's 2009 Survey," found at www.leadnet.org.
7. Michael Useem, Leading Up: How to Lead Your Boss So You Both Win (New York: Three Rivers Press, 2001) 2-6.

Chapter 5: Staff Team Design and Function

1. "Staff," http://dictionary.reference.com/browse/staff.
2. "Staff," http://dictionary.infoplease.com/staff.
3. *American Congregations 2008* is the report on the Faith Communities Today 2008 (FACT 2008) national survey of congregations conducted by the Cooperative Congregational Studies Partnership (CCSP). CCSP is a multi-faith coalition of denominations and religious groups hosted by the Hartford Institute for Religion Research, Hartford Seminary. *American Congregations 2008* was written by David A. Roozen, Director, The Hartford Institute for Religion Research, Professor of Religion & Society, Hartford Seminary, and Director, CCSP. http://hirr.hartsem.edu/about/roozen.htm.
4. Leadership Network, "Lean Staffing: Churches That Handle Staff Costs in Under 35% of Budget" by Warren Bird, Ph.D. Published on June 15, 2010 at http://leadnet.org/resources/download/lean_staffing_churches_that_handle_staff_costs_in_under_35_of_budget/
5. Martin Anderson, *Multiple Ministries* (Minneapolis: Augsburg, 1965), 5.
6. Lyle Schaller, *The Multiple Staff and the Larger Church* (Nashville: Abingdon, 1985), 59.
7. Gary McIntosh, *Staff Your Church for Growth* (Grand Rapids, Baker Books, 2000), 40.

Chapter 6: Governance and Board Function

1. Diane J. Duca, Nonprofit *Boards: Roles, Responsibilities and Performance* (New York: John Wiley and Sons, 1996), 3–4.
2. John Carver, *Boards That Make a Difference: A New Design for Leadership in Nonprofit and Public Organizations* (San Francisco: Jossey-Bass, 1997), 9–10.
3. Richard Chait, William Ryan, Barbara Taylor, *Governance as Leadership: Reframing the Work of Nonprofit Boards* (Hoboken, NJ: John Wiley and Sons, 2005), 6–10.
4. The term *trustee* denotes a person who holds assets for the benefit of another. In nonprofit organizations, a board holds assets in trust for the congregation. (Chait, 35.)
5. Chait, Ryan and Taylor, 51–52.
6. Ibid., 79–80.
7. Dan Hotchkiss, *Governance and Ministry: Rethinking Board Leadership* (Herndon, VA: The Alban Institute, 2009).
8. Ibid., 58.

9. Ibid., 66.
10. Ibid., 66.
11. Ibid., 59.
12. Ibid., 61–62.
13. Ibid., 93–100.
14. "The Consent Agenda: A Tool for Improving Governance," http://www.boardsource.org/dl.asp?document_id=484.
15. The reader who is interested in learning more about creating a performance management system that incorporates essential functions, core competencies, and performance goals is directed to *When Moses Meets Aaron: Staffing and Supervision in the Large Congregation* by Gil Rendle and Susan Beaumont (Herndon, VA: The Alban Institute, 2007).
16. This description of the role of the personnel committee originally appeared in the Fall 2009 issue of *Congregations*, published by the Alban Institute.

Chapter 7: Acculturation and Engagement of the Laity

1. Malcolm Gladwell, *The Tipping Point: How Little Things Can Make a Big Difference* (New York: Little, Brown and Company, 2000).
2. Arlin J. Rothauge, "Sizing Up a Congregation for New Member Ministry" (New York: Episcopal Church Center, 1983).
3. Robert Bast, *Attracting New Members* (Monrovia, CA: Church Growth Inc., 1988).
4. Owen Facey, *A Guide to Assimilation in the Local Church: Improving Your Church's Retention Capacity* (Bloomington, IN: First Books Publishing, 2002).
5. Taylor Cox Jr. and Ruby L. Beale, Developing *Competency to Manage Diversity* (San Francisco: Berrett-Koehler Publishers, Inc. 1997), 205.
6. Ibid., 204.
7. Roy M. Oswald and Speed B. Leas, *The Inviting Church: A Study of New Member Assimilation* (Bethesda, MD: The Alban Institute, 1987), 74–75.
8. Robert Schnase, *Five Practices of Fruitful Congregations* (Nashville: Abingdon Press, 2007), 11.
9. Edgar H. Schein, *Organizational Culture and Leadership*, 2nd Ed. (San Francisco: Jossey-Bass Publishers, 1992), 17–27.

Chapter 8: Forming and Executing Strategy

1. Richard Hughes and Katherine Beatty, *Becoming a Strategic Leader: Your Role in Your Organization's Success* (San Francisco: Jossey-Bass, 2005), 9.
2. Gil Rendle and Alice Mann, *Holy Conversations: Strategic Planning as a Spiritual Practice for Congregations* (Herndon, VA: The Alban Institute 2003), pages 3–6.
3. Mark Morgan, Raymond E. Levitt, and William Malek, *Executing Your Strategy: How to Break It Down and Get It Done* (Boston: Harvard Business School Press, 2007), 18.
4. Rendle and Mann, *Holy Conversations,* 85.
5. Ibid., 3–6.
6. U.S. Congregations is a religious research group staffed by religious researchers and sociologists who are conducting the U.S. Congregational Life Survey. It is housed in the offices of the Presbyterian Church (U.S.A.) in Louisville, Kentucky. You can read more about U.S. Congregation and see a sample copy of the survey at http://www.uscongregations.org/
7. Sarah Drummond, *Holy Clarity: The Practice of Planning and Evaluation* (Herndon, VA: The Alban Institute, 2009), xiii.
8. Jill M. Hudson, *Evaluating Ministry: Principles and Processes for Clergy and Congregations* (Herndon, VA: The Alban Institute, 1992).
9. Gil Rendle and Susan Beaumont, *When Moses Meets Aaron: Staffing and Supervision in the Large Congregation.* (Herndon, VA: The Alban Institute, 2007).
10. Kathleen A. Cahalan, *Projects that Matter: Successful Planning and Evaluation for Religious Organizations* (Bethesda, MD: Alban Institute, 2003), 9.